# Vegan
# THANKSGIVING
# DINNER & PIES

**AUDREY DUNHAM**

# *Vegan*
# THANKSGIVING
# DINNER & PIES

*All of your favorite Thanksgiving dinner and dessert classics made vegan!*

# SPECIAL THANKS AND DEDICATION

A big, loving thank you to my Mom, Dad, Grandma Norma, Grandma Phyllis, Grandpa John, Grandpa Clyde, Aunt Ellen, Uncle Craig, and Uncle Johnny for preparing and hosting incredible and wonderfully delicious Thanksgiving feasts throughout my life. My heart is warmed with so many happy memories of Thanksgivings past, which were truly an inspiration while creating this cookbook.

To Jeff, my soulmate, my partner in crime, the love of my life: Thank you for your unending encouragement, love, and support each and every day. I'm truly the luckiest lady alive because I have you by my side.

To my Thanksgiving recipe tasters and testers, Jeff, James, Jack, Mom, Dad, Emily, Tim, Berta, and Ashlyn, every note given was valuable and appreciated more than you know. Thank you, thank you, thank you!

This book is dedicated to my friend Lisa Karlan.
The world is a better place because you're in it.

Published by Audrey Dunham Celebrations™, an imprint of Audrey Dunham, Inc.

The scanning, uploading, and distribution of this book without permission is theft of the author's intellectual property. If you would like permission to use materials from this book (other than for review purposes) please contact audrey@audreydunham.com. Thank you for your support of the author's rights.

**Audrey Dunham Celebrations™**

13801 Ventura Blvd.
Sherman Oaks, CA 91423

Instagram and Facebook: @AudreyDunham

First Edition: October 2021

**Book cover and design:** Katherine Case

**Food photography:** Vanessa Stump

**Food and prop styling:** Vanessa Stump, Audrey Dunham, and Chris Hatcher

**Editing:** Christine McKnight

**Indexing:** Rudy Leon

ISBNs: 978-1-7367601-1-6 (hardcover) and 978-1-7367601-2-3 (ebook)

Library of Congress Control Number: 2021914442

Publisher's Cataloging-In-Publication Data (Prepared by The Donohue Group, Inc.)

Names: Dunham, Audrey, author.

Title: Vegan Thanksgiving dinner & pies : all your favorite Thanksgiving dinner and dessert classics made vegan! / Audrey Dunham.

Other Titles: Vegan Thanksgiving dinner and pies

Description: First edition. | Sherman Oaks, California : Audrey Dunham Celebrations, an imprint of Audrey Dunham, Inc., 2021. | Includes index.

Identifiers: ISBN 9781736760116 (hardcover) | ISBN 9781736760123 (ebook)

Subjects: LCSH: Thanksgiving cooking. | Vegan cooking. | Dinners and dining. | Pies. | LCGFT: Cookbooks.

Classification: LCC TX739.2.T45 D86 2021 (print) | LCC TX739.2.T45 (ebook) | DDC 641.568--dc23

# CONTENTS

# INTRODUCTION

**Autumn is such a glorious and special time of year. The weather begins cooling down, the leaves outside change to shades of yellow, orange, and crimson red, and it's the season that hosts the beloved holiday we call Thanksgiving.**

Though there are a handful of other grand, celebratory meals throughout the year that we look forward to, there's nothing quite like Thanksgiving dinner. The menu hardly varies from year to year, so our memories spark feelings of joy and excitement as we imagine our plates piled high with all the classics we know and love. Personally, taking that first bite of pumpkin pie (generously topped with whipped cream) on Thanksgiving Day is a moment I dream about all year!

In creating this cookbook, my main mission was to provide "veganized" recipes for everyone's favorite Thanksgiving dishes and pies that taste just as good as, if not better than, the traditional versions. Keeping this in mind, I didn't hold back. Ingredients were used in abundance, as I aimed to pack as much flavor, richness, and oh-wow deliciousness as I could into each and every recipe.

After all, eating a dairy-, egg-, or meat-free diet, whether by necessity or by choice, certainly doesn't equal a life free of fantastic, indulgent, or incredible meals. In my experience, it's quite the opposite. When I chose this path for myself, my eyes were opened to ingredients that had previously gone ignored. I was encouraged to think outside the box and explore new culinary possibilities, and my tastebuds have never been happier.

In the pages that follow, you'll find recipes for all of the classic Thanksgiving dishes and pies: fluffy mashed potatoes, stuffing, sky-high biscuits, gravy, mac and cheese, apple, pecan, and pumpkin pies, and of course, the coveted "turkey" roast.

However, you'll also see new options to consider for your Thanksgiving table, particularly in the Mains section of this book. There's a Mushroom Wellington (my husband, Jeff's, favorite), a Stuffing-Stuffed Whole Roasted Cauliflower (one of my personal favorites), a luxurious Butternut Squash Lasagna, a flavor-loaded Baked Bean Cornbread Casserole, and so much more.

Oh, and be sure to keep an eye out for some surprises in the Pies section, too—particularly the Caramel Apple Crumble Slab Pie and Chocolate Cream Pie with Chocolate Cookie Crust. *Yum.*

Truly, an abundance of thought and love went into each and every recipe in this cookbook. I hope you and yours love these recipes just as much as I have loved creating them!

**My sincerest wish for you is that this cookbook evokes the excitement of preparing and serving an incredible Thanksgiving feast, this year and every year after.**

# TIPS FOR BEING THE ULTIMATE HOST

Hosting Thanksgiving dinner, no matter the size of the group you're having over, is a big responsibility and requires a lot of time and energy. It can certainly feel a bit overwhelming at times, especially during those final hours just before serving.

Therefore, I felt it was important to include a section in this book dedicated to the art of hosting. Here you'll discover ways to not only make Thanksgiving feel much more manageable for you, but also to make the day feel especially memorable for your guests.

## Tip # 1 - Make plans and lists.

**Two weeks before Thanksgiving,** sit down and plan out your menu for the big feast. Sometimes I like to text my guests (even if it's simply close family members) and ask what dish or dishes are their favorites so I can be sure to include them. Our menu usually includes the following:

- A main dish (varies from year to year)
- Gravy
- A mashed potato dish
- A stuffing
- A sweet potato dish
- Two to three vegetables
- Bread (rolls, biscuits, or cornbread)
- Cranberry sauce
- Plain as well as flavored butter
- Two to four pies
- Vanilla ice cream
- Whipped cream

Don't forget to include beverages on your written menu. My beverage list usually includes:

- A pitcher or dispenser of ice water with orange or lemon slices
- Champagne or a specialty autumn-inspired cocktail for a pre-meal drink
- Sparkling apple cider, warm mulled cider, fruit juice, or sodas for young guests or those avoiding alcohol
- White and red wine to serve with the meal
- Plain ice water (no citrus added) to serve with the meal
- Regular or decaf coffee to serve with dessert, plus any creamer or milk
- Plenty of ice for serving in drinks and keeping champagne, white wine, and nonalcoholic drinks cold

Finally, I'll also include some very light appetizers or snacks on the menu for guests to nibble on before the meal, such as bowls of salted mixed nuts and a colorful crudite platter with dip. I typically don't do much more than that—after all, we don't want to oversaturate our tastebuds before sitting down for one of the most decadent and flavorful meals we'll have all year!

Once you have a solid menu in place including all dishes, desserts, drinks, and light appetizers, I recommend making one giant grocery list. Divide your grocery list into three categories based on where each item can be found in the grocery store:

**Produce and Bakery Sections**

**Dry Goods** (shelf-stable items that do not need to be kept cold)

**Refrigerator and Freezer Sections**

As you go through each recipe on your menu, write down each ingredient you need under the proper category on your grocery list. Dividing up your grocery list into these three categories will keep you organized, save your sanity in the store, and make shopping a total breeze.

Typically, I'll buy every item listed in my Dry Goods category two weeks in advance. Then I'll revisit the store for the items in the Produce / Bakery and Refrigerator / Freezer categories about four days before Thanksgiving so they're nice and fresh.

Note: Now is a good time to check the expiration dates on all your spices and dried herbs. They typically begin to lose their flavor three to six months after opening, depending on the spice or herb.

**One week before Thanksgiving,** write out a seven-day execution plan that counts down to the big day.

One of the biggest mistakes a host can make is attempting to put the entire meal together within a 10–12 hour period. It's important to know that not every dish and dessert needs to be prepared on Thanksgiving Day to taste fresh and extraordinary. In fact, there are some that truly need to be made one day prior (such as most pies in this book), while others, such as stuffing and casseroles, can be assembled up to three days in advance and then baked just before serving.

To assist with making this execution plan, each recipe in this cookbook has a "Make-Ahead Tip" at the bottom. Read them carefully to see what can be done in advance and what needs to be done just before serving.

On your execution plan, you'll also want to designate a day for setting your dining room table and choosing serving dishes and serving spoons. Put sticky notes on each one to remember what dish will go with which recipe.

Here's a basic example of what my seven-day execution plan might look like:

**7 days out:**
• Tidy up the house, removing any unwanted paper piles and such
• Clear out the coat closet so guests have a place to put coats and purses
• Figure out your music situation—make a playlist or choose a station to listen to

**6 days out:**
• Set the dining room table
• Polish water and wine glasses
• Choose serving dishes and spoons and polish as needed

**5 days out:**
• Make ice cream
• Choose wine and add more to grocery list, if needed
• Make a flavored butter or two

**4 days out:**
• Shop for Produce / Bakery section and Refrigerator / Freezer section items
• Chop bread for stuffing and leave bread cubes out to become stale
• Chop potatoes for mashed potatoes

**3 days out:**
• Assemble stuffing
• Make cranberry sauce
• Assemble sweet potato dish

**2 days out:**
• Chop vegetables
• Make pie crusts
• Make salad dressing

**1 day out:**
• Bake pies
• Make vegan roast

**Thanksgiving Day:**

**10:00 a.m.** - Bake cornbread muffins

**10:30 a.m.** - Chop veggies for the crudité platter

**11:30 a.m.** - Chop greens for the salad

**12:00 p.m.** - Eat lunch

**1:00 p.m.** - Gather ingredients for gravy, mac and cheese, sautéed green beans, or any other last-minute recipes

**2:00 p.m.** - Put water and coffee grounds in the coffee maker, put drinks on ice

**2:30 p.m.** - Get myself and the kids ready

**3:30 p.m.** - Place light appetizers on tables and counters, add water, ice, and sliced lemon to drink dispenser, set up the drink station

**4:00 p.m.** - Light candles and start the music, pull all casseroles and stuffing from the fridge to sit at room temperature

**4:15- 4:30 p.m.** - Greet guests as they arrive, open wine needed for the meal

**4:30 p.m.** - Make mac and cheese, start boiling potatoes

**4:45 p.m.** - Mash potatoes, remove butters from the fridge

**5:00 p.m.** - Place vegetables, casseroles, and stuffing in the oven to roast / bake

**5:10 p.m.** - Make gravy, reheat vegan roast, and remove pies from the fridge

**5:30 p.m.** - Assemble salad, remove cranberry sauce from the fridge

**5:45 p.m.** - Dinner time!

Some tasks will likely overlap here and there, but having this list on your counter on a piece of paper or on several sticky notes will truly make your Thanksgiving feel seamless and easy.

## Tip #2 - Take people up on their offer to help, as most people truly want to!

This one is simple, and is especially true for the items on your execution list for Thanksgiving Day. Have someone light the candles for you, open wine bottles, or even whisk the gravy. People feel good when they know they are contributing and being helpful.

The same goes for preparing all of the dishes. If a family member or friend offers to bring a pie or side dish, take them up on the offer!

## Tip #3 - Make your guests feel welcome the moment they arrive.

There are plenty of ways to make your guests feel special on Thanksgiving, many of which require little effort. Here are some examples:

• Make your front door or porch look festive. A simple fall wreath, an autumn welcome sign, or a few pumpkins placed near the entry go a long way in making your guests feel welcomed and excited to enter your home.

• Light candles in all the main areas of the house, including the guest bathroom, sitting areas, and of course the dining room table. Note: I recommend unscented candles everywhere except perhaps the guest bathroom, as scented candles will compete with the glorious smells of your food.

• Have music playing to set the mood. We're big fans of music from Sinatra's era when entertaining in our home.

• Show guests a designated area for hanging coats and keeping purses, such as a hall closet. Take it one step further by offering to hang the coat for them!

• After coats and purses have been put away, immediately let guests know the drink options and offer to pour their first drink. I like to set up a little drink station (usually someplace away from the kitchen and the main fridge) so everyone can easily help themselves to refills throughout the evening.

• Set place markers for everyone at the dining room table(s) when hosting larger groups. This is especially helpful when hosting a mix of friends and family in an effort to avoid any awkward feelings of "where in the world should I sit?" Be thoughtful when choosing each person's spot and consider where they'll likely be most comfortable. Just be sure to assign each seat *before* guests arrive.

## Tip #4 - Give your guests something fun to do before the meal.

• A simple activity or game can be a great icebreaker before everyone sits down to dinner. For example, one year my husband, Jeff, bought a Polaroid camera and told each guest that they were going to have their picture taken, but their job was to choose one random item in our house to hold in their photo! This ended up being really fun, and the items some people chose to hold were downright hilarious. Afterward, Jeff took everyone's photos and placed them on small card stands on the table to mark each person's seat. We all talked about and laughed at those photos for the rest of the night. I truly applaud Jeff for coming up with such a fun idea!

• Give the younger guests an activity to do, too. Lay white butcher paper across the kids' table and set out cups holding washable markers of every color. They'll have a ball drawing turkeys and happy faces and writing their names in big letters at their spots. If the kids are sitting at the big table with the adults, instead lay white paper placemats out for them to color on.

Alternatively (or in addition), you can download and print out paper pilgrim or turkey hats for the kids to cut out and put together. Afterward, they'll have something fun and silly to wear the rest of the night.

Jeff chose to hold a box of his favorite childhood cereal for his photo!

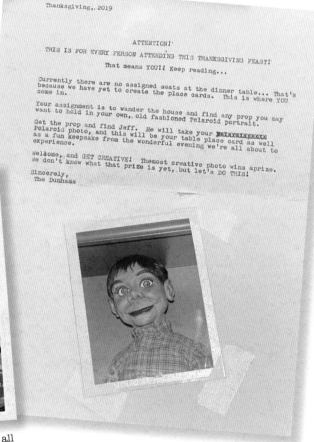

Thanksgiving, 2019

ATTENTION!
THIS IS FOR EVERY PERSON ATTENDING THIS THANKSGIVING FEAST!

That means YOU!! Keep reading...

Currently there are no assigned seats at the dinner table... That's because we have yet to create the place cards. This is where YOU come in.

Your assignment is to wander the house and find any prop you may want to hold in your own, old fashioned Polaroid portrait.

Get the prop and find Jeff. He will take your XXXXXXXXXXXX Polaroid photo, and this will be your table place card as well as a fun keepsake from the wonderful evening we're all about to experience.

Welcome, and GET CREATIVE! The most creative photo wins a prize. We don't know what that prize is yet, but let's DO THIS!

Sincerely,
The Dunhams

James opted to hold a toy firetruck, all while making the goofiest smile ever!

## Tip #5 - Don't drink alcohol while you cook!

Others may argue, but alcohol and cooking a big meal don't mix. Chances are, that glass of champagne will throw off your judgment and your timing, which can lead to overcooking and other mistakes. If you're planning to drink, I truly recommend waiting to have that first sip until you sit down at the dinner table to eat.

## Tip #6 - If possible, create a buffet rather than serving family-style.

After hosting many holiday meals, I know this for sure: people would much rather fill their plates at a buffet than have to awkwardly pass platters and hot dishes around a table. Also, I've noticed people almost never have seconds when food is served family-style. But when food is served buffet-style (preferably in a separate room away from the dining room, such as the kitchen), guests are much more likely to get up for seconds.

## Tip #7 - Make a thoughtful toast.

Recognize the reason for the holiday and show gratitude for the guests by mentioning each person in a short yet thoughtful toast just before or during dinner. Thank them for joining you on this holiday, tell them how much it means to you to have them there, and perhaps share how each person has made your life better. This is the ultimate way to make your guests feel special on Thanksgiving.

## Tip #8 - Make a little more food than you need, knowing people love leftovers!

If you're questioning whether or not to double a recipe or make that extra pie, I would encourage you to absolutely do it. One of the best parts of Thanksgiving is the leftovers, and it's always better to have extra than to not have enough (or in this case—just enough!).

## Tip #9 - Provide brand-new takeout or storage containers for your guests so they can easily take leftovers home.

This is such a simple and inexpensive way to make Thanksgiving feel special for your guests. And in the end, they'll be able to continue enjoying your cooking throughout the holiday weekend!

Of course, I chose to hold one of my freshly-baked pies.

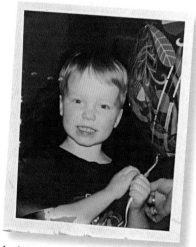

And Jack went with a Thanksgiving balloon for his photo!

# LET'S TALK INGREDIENTS

**When it comes to vegan (dairy-free) butter or margarine,** I prefer one that has vegetable oil or vegetable oil blend listed as the first ingredient rather than coconut oil. The overall flavor and texture of vegetable oil–based butter seems to work better in the recipes. In addition, I always use butters that are salted rather than unsalted.

If your butter doesn't state whether it's salted on the front of the package, simply look to the ingredients to make sure salt is listed. However, if you only have unsalted butter on hand, I recommend adding an additional ¼ teaspoon of salt for every ½ cup of butter called for in the recipe.

**To soften your butter more quickly for use,** try this method: slice or scoop your butter by the tablespoon and place the 1-tablespoon pieces into a microwave-safe bowl, separating the pieces as much as possible from one another. Heat in the microwave for just 10 seconds. If your butter is still cold, heat for another 5 seconds. This should do the trick! Another method is to grate sticks or large mounds of butter on the largest holes of a grater and then allow it to sit at room temperature on a plate or in a bowl until soft.

**When it comes to choosing which type of oil to use,** I recommend opting for neutral-flavored oils such as canola, safflower, or sunflower, to name a few. Unless specified in the recipe, refrain from using olive oil or coconut oil, as they may affect the flavor and/or texture of the finished recipe. Avocado oil has a lovely, buttery quality to it, but it's best used in recipes that are heated below 400°F (about 204°C).

**If you'd like to make your recipes gluten free,** look at the bottom of each recipe to see my recommendations on how to go about it. Oftentimes, the best method is simply swapping out regular all-purpose flour for gluten free all-purpose flour, garbanzo bean (chickpea) flour, or a certain type of starch. But there are several recipes in this book that I feel do best with xanthan gum added, as well. Read the notes for Best Gluten Free Version at the bottom of each recipe for details.

**Dried herbs can be an easy, time-saving alternative to fresh herbs,** but every now and then a recipe comes along that truly turns out better when the fresh types are used. In this cookbook, simply look to the ingredient lists to see which ones require fresh herbs, which require dried herbs, or if you have the option to use either one.

**Dairy-free chocolate chips can sometimes be hard to find,** so for the pies that require chocolate in this cookbook, chocolate chips can be replaced with chocolate chunks or chopped chocolate bar. I recommend tasting all chocolate before using it in your recipes to make sure you like the flavor. The flavor of unpleasant-tasting chocolate can't be hidden in pies or any other dessert, and will come through in the end result.

**If you prefer using frozen store-bought pie crust to save time, that is perfectly fine.** I find most of them are naturally vegan and have a pretty good flavor and texture. However, there are two things to keep in mind if you decide to go this route. First, typically the frozen crusts that come in disposable plates do not need to be par-baked in recipes such as Pumpkin Pie, even if the frozen crust says to do so in its instructions. I find they often burn or become too firm after the finished pie comes out of the oven. Therefore, I recommend skipping that step and adding the filling to a raw, thawed crust instead.

Second, frozen pie crusts that come in disposable plates tend to hold less filling than a pie crust made from scratch and molded to a 9-inch (about 23-cm) pie plate by hand. Therefore, be careful not to overfill your frozen pie crust when adding your filling. It's better to have leftover pumpkin pie custard or buttermilk custard than to have a pie that overflows.

**Let's talk about non-dairy milk.** Gone are the days of soy as the only non-dairy milk choice! At this point in time, there are countless non-dairy milks made from a variety of plant-based foods. I will say, however, when it comes to using them in recipes, there are a few that I prefer over others.

In my experience, the milks that work best are those that have low to moderate amounts of fats and carbohydrates (about 4 grams or less per 1 cup/237 ml). For example, oat milk is a big favorite among non-dairy milk drinkers and I certainly love it too, but it typically contains high amounts of both carbohydrates, from the oats, and fats, from the oil usually added by the manufacturer. The quantity of carbs and fats in this type of milk can negatively affect the results of a recipe, altering the texture and look of the finished product.

A higher amount of protein, on the other hand, as in soy milk for example, does not seem to negatively affect the results of a recipe. In fact, the higher amounts of protein can be helpful with recipes that require a lot of structure, such as breads. I would, however, avoid using the milks with high amounts of *added* protein, to play it safe.

When it comes down to it, I opt for an unsweetened, unflavored almond, cashew, or soy milk containing 25–70 calories per 1 cup (237 ml). The calorie count is a nice and easy number check, as any number higher than 70 usually indicates the milk is high in carbs and/or fats.

For those who have allergies to both nuts and soy, my fourth choice at this point in time is a low-fat oat milk. It may be higher in carbohydrates, but at least it's lower in fats.

# MY TOP COOKING TIPS

**Before starting any recipe,** it's best to create your mise en place (MEEZ ahn plahs), which is a French term for having all your ingredients prepped and measured out into separate bowls. Mixing bowls, tools, and equipment should be set out as well. Taking the time to do this before you start baking or cooking ensures that you'll have the correct amount of each ingredient, and helps make the recipe execution process easier and more fluid once you begin.

**For the most accurate ingredient measuring,** I recommend using a food scale for all dry ingredients used in quantities of 1 tablespoon and up. As you'll see, I included grams as well as cup measurements in this cookbook. But since cup measurements can vary ever so slightly depending on how tightly a measuring cup is packed or how densely an ingredient sits in its package, the only true way to know if you're adding the intended amount is by weighing. The extra bonus is, your cleanup will be minimal; in the end you'll have just one bowl to wash vs. several dirty measuring cups!

**If you choose to use measuring cups,** I recommend using the scoop-and-sweep method for all powdery dry ingredients such as flour or starch. For this method, first use a fork or whisk to fluff up the top layers of the ingredient within the package to help loosen it before measuring, then take your measuring cup and scoop out a heaping amount. Using the back flat edge of a table knife or a very straight index finger, level off the top so it is even with the perimeter of the cup.

**In pie recipes, you'll see that I recommend placing each pie on a baking sheet before putting it in the oven.** This is simply for easier pie handling and to ensure your crust doesn't get damaged by a potholder while going in or coming out of the oven.

# MAINS

# MUSHROOM WELLINGTON

*It seems any recipe that involves puff pastry is sure to be a winner, and this mushroom Wellington is truly no exception. Aside from its light and crispy exterior, this Wellington's minced mushroom center is loaded with layers of flavors, including sage, thyme, onion, and a slight balsamic sweet tang. This is one of my husband, Jeff's, most favorite recipes.*

YIELD: ABOUT 6 SERVINGS

INGREDIENTS:

- 1 sheet frozen vegan puff pastry
- 1 lb. (454 g) white mushrooms
- 3 ½ Tbsp. (53 ml) olive oil or avocado oil, divided
- 2 c. (256 g) chopped red onion
- 3 medium cloves garlic, minced
- 2 Tbsp. (30 ml) balsamic vinegar
- ½ c. (70 g) chopped home-cooked or canned water chestnuts (optional)
- ½ Tbsp. chopped fresh thyme (or ½ tsp. dried thyme)
- ½ Tbsp. chopped fresh sage (or ½ tsp. dried sage)
- ¾ tsp. salt, plus more to taste
- ¼ tsp. black pepper, plus more to taste
- 4 oz. (113 g) fresh baby spinach, roughly chopped
- ½ Tbsp. unsweetened, unflavored non-dairy milk

FOR BEST GLUTEN FREE VERSION:
Use gluten free frozen puff pastry.

MAKE-AHEAD TIP:
The mushroom mixture (steps 3–6) can be prepared up to 2 days in advance. Cool for 15 minutes before storing in the fridge in an airtight container. When needed, allow the mixture to sit at room temperature for 30–45 minutes before adding to the center of your puff pastry. Complete all the remaining steps just before serving.

INSTRUCTIONS:

1. Preheat your oven to 375°F (approx. 190°C). Line a baking sheet with parchment paper.

2. Take the puff pastry out of the freezer and set aside to thaw.

3. Place the mushrooms in the bowl of a food processor and pulse until crumbly, 10–11 times. Do not over process.

4. Heat 2 Tbsp. (30 ml) of the oil in a large skillet over medium-high heat. Add the onion and sauté until soft, 3–4 minutes. Lower the heat to medium and add the garlic. Sauté for an additional 2 minutes.

5. Add the mushrooms and balsamic vinegar and cook, stirring occasionally, until most of the liquid from the mushrooms has evaporated, 10–12 minutes.

6. Push the mushroom mixture to the side of the skillet and add 1 Tbsp. of oil (15 ml) to the center. Add the water chestnuts, if using, and the thyme, sage, salt, and pepper and sauté until the herbs are fragrant, about 1 minute. Add the spinach and stir until wilted. Incorporate this spinach mixture into the mushroom mixture. Turn off the heat and add more salt and pepper to taste.

7. Roll out the puff pastry on a lightly floured flat surface so the pastry extends an additional 1–2 inches (2.5–5 cm) in each of the four directions. Transfer to your parchment-lined baking sheet.

8. Add the mushroom mixture to the center of the pastry and form into a loaf shape. Fold both of the long sides up to meet in the center and pinch to seal the two together. Trim any excess pastry off the two short ends so you're left with roughly 1 ½ inches (about 4 cm) of pastry on either side. (The trimmed pieces of puff pastry dough can be used to make a decorative braid or design and placed on top of the Wellington just before baking.) Take the two short ends and fold them up and over the top of the Wellington. Gently turn the loaf over so all seams are now underneath.

9. Using a very sharp knife, score two rows of 1-inch (2.5-cm) diagonal slits across the top of the Wellington. Pierce a few small holes in each side, as well.

10. Combine the remaining ½ Tbsp. of oil and the milk in a small bowl and brush a light coating over the entire surface of the Wellington.

11. Bake for 40–45 minutes, or until golden brown, rotating the baking sheet at the 20-minute mark. Let rest 10 minutes before slicing into thick slices.

# STUFFING-STUFFED WHOLE ROASTED CAULIFLOWER

*This dish is a true showstopper thanks to the sheer uniqueness of a whole roasted cauliflower, complete with a crispy golden exterior. The "wow" factor is taken to the next level once you slice into it to reveal savory stuffing nestled within the florets.*

YIELD: 6–8 SERVINGS

INGREDIENTS:

- 2 Tbsp. + ½ tsp. salt, divided
- 1 (2 ½–3-lb. / 1134–1361-g) head cauliflower
- ¼ c. (23 g) panko breadcrumbs
- ⅓ c. + 1 Tbsp. (85 g) vegan butter or margarine, melted and divided
- 3 Tbsp. (15 g) nutritional yeast flakes
- 1 tsp. onion powder, divided
- ½ tsp. garlic powder, divided
- ¼ tsp. black pepper, divided
- 2 slices white bread, toasted
- ¼ c. (59 ml) low-sodium vegetable broth
- 1 stalk celery, chopped into pea-sized pieces
- ½ tsp. dried thyme
- ½ tsp. dried sage
- ½ tsp. curry powder

FOR BEST GLUTEN FREE VERSION:
Use gluten free bread in place of the white bread, and use gluten free breadcrumbs in place of the regular (the panko type, if possible).

MAKE-AHEAD TIP:
The stuffing (steps 6 and 7) can be made up to 3 days in advance and stored in an airtight container in the fridge. Allow the stuffing to sit at room temperature for 30 minutes before stuffing inside the cauliflower.

INSTRUCTIONS:

1. Preheat your oven to 400°F (approx. 204°C) and position a rack in the center of the oven. Line a baking sheet with parchment paper and set aside.

2. Fill a large stock pot two-thirds full with water and add 2 Tbsp. of the salt. Bring the water to a boil over high heat.

3. Meanwhile, carefully trim away the cauliflower leaves and stem without cutting any florets.

4. Boil the cauliflower, stem side up, just until slightly tender, 4–5 minutes depending on the size of the cauliflower. Carefully remove the head and allow it to cool and drain on a clean kitchen towel, stem side down.

5. In a small bowl, combine the breadcrumbs, 2 Tbsp. (28 g) of the melted butter, the nutritional yeast, ½ tsp. onion powder, ¼ tsp. garlic powder, ¼ tsp. salt, and ⅛ tsp. pepper. Set aside.

6. Finely chop the two pieces of white toast into ¼-inch (0.5-cm) cubes and transfer to a small mixing bowl. Drizzle 2 Tbsp. (28 g) of the melted butter evenly over the cubes.

7. Add the vegetable broth, celery, thyme, sage, curry powder, and the remaining ½ tsp. onion powder, ¼ tsp. garlic powder, ¼ tsp. salt, and ⅛ tsp. pepper to the mixing bowl. Mash the ingredients together with the back of a spoon until it resembles very moist stuffing. Add this stuffing mixture to a piping bag and cut off the tip to create roughly a ½-inch (about 1.5-cm) opening.

8. Turn the cauliflower stem side up and pipe the stuffing between the stalks of the cauliflower, pushing it as far as it can possibly go in every direction with your fingertips as you go. Be sure to use all of the stuffing.

9. Transfer the cauliflower to the prepared baking sheet, stem side down. Brush with the remaining 2 Tbsp. (28 g) melted butter and press the breadcrumb mixture evenly over the surface.

10. Bake until fork-tender and the breadcrumbs are a deep golden brown, 35–40 minutes for larger-sized heads (30–35 minutes for a medium-sized head). Rest 5-10 minutes before slicing into wedges.

# HOLIDAY "TURKEY" ROAST

*This roast will satisfy both the veggie lovers and omnivores in your group with its use of herbs and spices and its sliceable, meat-like texture. I will say, my favorite part of all is the flavor-blasting savory-sweet glaze applied at the end that gives an enticing look to this roast. (The gluten free version of this recipe on the following page includes a similar glaze.) Serve with brown gravy, if you like.*

YIELD: ABOUT 6 SERVINGS

INGREDIENTS:

- 1 (15-oz. / 425-g) can garbanzo beans (chickpeas), drained and rinsed
- 4 ½ c. (1067 ml) low-sodium vegetable broth, or more as needed, divided
- 2 Tbsp. (30 ml) neutral-flavored oil
- 1 Tbsp. (15 ml) soy sauce or substitute
- 1 Tbsp. (15 g) tomato paste
- 2 Tbsp. (10 g) nutritional yeast flakes
- 2 tsp. onion powder
- 1 tsp. garlic powder
- 1 tsp. salt
- 1 tsp. dried sage
- ¾ tsp. dried thyme
- ½ tsp. curry powder
- ¼ tsp. dried rosemary
- 1 ½ c. (234 g) vital wheat gluten

Glaze:
- 2 Tbsp. (30 ml) neutral-flavored oil
- 2 Tbsp. (30 ml) maple syrup
- 2 tsp. soy sauce or substitute

FOR BEST GLUTEN FREE VERSION:
See the recipe for Gluten Free Holiday "Turkey" Roast on page 28.

MAKE-AHEAD TIP:
The roast can be formed and steamed (steps 1–5) 1 day in advance. Allow roast to cool for 15 minutes and then place in the fridge in an airtight container or wrapped with two layers of plastic wrap. When needed, allow the roast to rest at room temperature for 30 minutes before following steps 6–8.

INSTRUCTIONS:

1. In the bowl of a food processor, combine the garbanzo beans, ¾ c. (177 ml) of the vegetable broth, the oil, soy sauce, tomato paste, nutritional yeast flakes, onion and garlic powders, salt, sage, thyme, curry powder, and rosemary. Blend until very smooth, scraping the sides and bottom as needed.

2. Transfer this mixture to a large mixing bowl. Add the vital wheat gluten and combine at first with a spoon or spatula, and then with your hands as the mixture becomes thick. Make sure all vital wheat gluten is incorporated into the dough.

3. Transfer the dough to a flat surface lightly dusted with additional vital wheat gluten. Knead the dough about 10 times, then shape into a loaf.

4. Line a large pot with a steamer basket (preferably a flat-bottomed one) and add just enough vegetable broth to rise about ½ inch (1 cm) above the steamer basket, 3 ½–3 ¾ c. (roughly 880 ml), depending on the size of your pot.

5. Place the loaf in the steamer basket and bring the broth to a boil over medium-high heat. Once boiling, cover the pot and reduce the heat to low to maintain a simmer. Steam the loaf for 1 hour, checking every 20 minutes to make sure the broth hasn't completely evaporated. Add additional hot broth to the pot if needed. Afterward, remove the lid and allow the roast to rest for 10 minutes.

6. Meanwhile, preheat your oven to 350°F (approx. 177°C) and line a baking sheet with parchment paper. When the roast has rested for 10 minutes, place it in the center of the prepared baking sheet.

7. In a ramekin or small bowl, stir together all ingredients for the glaze. Brush the entire surface of the roast (including the bottom) with the glaze several times until roughly half of the glaze mixture has been applied.

8. Place the roast in the oven and bake for 20 minutes. Remove from the oven and brush with all of the remaining glaze (skipping the bottom this time). Let rest for 10 minutes before slicing. Serve with gravy, if desired.

# GLUTEN FREE HOLIDAY "TURKEY" ROAST

*You'll be blown away by this incredibly simple holiday roast! It offers the traditional flavors of Thanksgiving with its abundance of herbs, all with the sliceable texture of baked tofu. Be sure to make two roasts if you're cooking for a crowd! Serve with brown gravy, if you like.*

YIELD: 3–4 SERVINGS

INGREDIENTS:

- 14 oz. (396 g) extra-firm tofu
- 2 Tbsp. (30 ml) neutral-flavored oil
- 1 Tbsp. (15 g) tomato paste
- 1 Tbsp. (15 ml) gluten free soy sauce or substitute
- 1 tsp. agar powder
- 1 vegetable bouillon cube (or 1 tsp. bouillon substitute)
- ¼ c. (30 g) tapioca starch
- ¼ c. (37 g) garbanzo bean (chickpea) flour
- 1 Tbsp. (5 g) nutritional yeast flakes
- 2 tsp. onion powder
- 1 ½ tsp. garlic powder
- ½ tsp. dried sage
- ½ tsp. curry powder
- ½ tsp. salt
- ¼ tsp. dried thyme
- ¼ tsp. dried rosemary

Glaze:

- 1 Tbsp. + 1 tsp. (20 ml) neutral-flavored oil
- 1 Tbsp. + 1 tsp. (20 ml) maple syrup
- 2 tsp. gluten free soy sauce or substitute

INSTRUCTIONS:

1. Preheat your oven to 350°F (approx. 177°C). Line a baking sheet with foil followed by a sheet of parchment paper right on top.

2. Drain the tofu, wrap it with several paper towels or a clean dish towel, and gently press to extract any excess liquid. Allow the wrapped tofu to sit at least 5 minutes.

3. In a small bowl, combine the oil, tomato paste, soy sauce, and agar and stir well. Add the bouillon and stir or mash it with a fork (if using the cubed type). Set aside for now.

4. In a mixing bowl, stir together the starch, chickpea flour, nutritional yeast, onion powder, garlic powder, sage, curry powder, salt, thyme, and rosemary.

5. Break the tofu into large chunks and place it in the bowl of a food processor, then add the wet ingredient mixture. Pulse until mostly combined. The mixture will appear crumbly.

6. Next, add the dry ingredients to the food processor and pulse again until well combined, scraping the sides and bottom as needed.

7. Transfer this soft dough to the center of your baking sheet, right on top of the parchment. Form a loaf shape roughly 4 inches (10 cm) wide by 7 inches (18 cm) long by 2–3 inches (5–7.5 cm) tall. Smooth over the surface as much as you can.

8. Pull the parchment paper tightly around the roast lengthwise, then twist and tuck under the two ends to secure them. Then, do the same with the foil, being careful not to smash the loaf.

9. Transfer to the oven and roast for 35 minutes. In the meantime, stir together the glaze ingredients in a small bowl.

**MAKE-AHEAD TIP:**
The roast can be made up to 2 days in advance and stored in an airtight container until needed. See step 12 for reheating instructions.

10. After 35 minutes, remove the roast from the oven and carefully pull the foil and parchment layers back and lay them flat. Brush the roast all over with half of the glaze mixture. Roast, uncovered, for an additional 35 minutes. Note: Store the remaining glaze in an airtight container and place in the fridge to be used just before serving.

11. Remove the roast from the oven and allow it to cool completely, then transfer it to an airtight container or wrap in two layers of plastic wrap. Place it in the fridge to chill for at least 6 hours or up to 2 days. (See second note below.)

12. To reheat for serving, allow the chilled roast to warm to room temperature for 45–60 minutes, then place on a parchment-lined or nonstick baking sheet. Heat the roast in a 350°F (approx. 177°C) oven for 20–25 minutes, or until hot. Brush roast with the remaining glaze, then let it rest for 5–10 minutes before slicing and serving.

**NOTES:**
- If you like the idea of a super simple soy-based roast but do not require it to be gluten free, ¼ c. (35 g) all-purpose flour can be used in place of the tapioca starch, and regular soy sauce can be used in place of the gluten free soy sauce.
- If you don't have time to chill the roast for at least 6 hours, that's ok! It can be topped with glaze and served after baking the initial 70 minutes. It will be slightly softer in this case, but delicious nonetheless.

# BUTTERNUT SQUASH LASAGNA

*Lasagna at Thanksgiving?! Well in this case, the answer is yes. When marinara sauce is replaced with a creamy butternut squash sauce with sage and basil and just a hint of holiday-inspired spices, you are warmed with the aromas and flavors of Thanksgiving from the inside out.*

YIELD: ABOUT 12 SERVINGS

INGREDIENTS:

**Butternut Squash Sauce:**
- 1 large butternut squash (about 3 lb./1360 g)
- 1 c. (237 ml) unsweetened, unflavored non-dairy milk
- 1 ½ Tbsp. (23 ml) maple syrup
- 1 ½ tsp. chopped fresh basil (or ½ tsp. dried basil)
- ¾ tsp. chopped fresh sage (or ¼ tsp. dried sage)
- 1 ½ tsp. salt
- ½ tsp. cinnamon
- ¼ tsp. allspice
- ¼ tsp. nutmeg
- ⅛ tsp. black pepper

**Cashew Ricotta Cream:**
- 1 ¾ c. + 2 Tbsp. (238 g) raw unsalted cashews
- 1 ¼ c. (296 ml) warm water, plus more water for boiling
- 2 ½ Tbsp. (13 g) nutritional yeast flakes
- 1 Tbsp + 1 tsp. (20 ml) lemon juice
- 1 ¼ tsp. salt
- ½ tsp. + 1 pinch garlic powder
- ⅛ tsp. + 1 pinch black pepper

**Spinach, Noodles, and Garnish:**
- 5 heaping c. (about 140 g) fresh baby spinach
- 1 Tbsp. (15 ml) olive oil, or 2–3 Tbsp. (30–45 ml) water
- Generous pinch each of salt and black pepper
- 8 lasagna noodles
- 3–4 fresh sage leaves, finely chopped for garnish

INSTRUCTIONS:

1. Preheat your oven to 375°F (approx. 190°C). Trim the ends off of the butternut squash, cut in half lengthwise, and scoop out the seeds with a spoon. Place the squash cut side down on a parchment-lined or nonstick baking sheet and roast for 40–60 minutes, or until the skin is shiny and browned and the squash is very soft and fork-tender. When done, remove the squash to cool, but leave the oven on.

2. Meanwhile, place the cashews in a medium-sized saucepan and cover with water. Bring to a boil over medium-high heat. Once boiling, continue cooking for 10 minutes. Reduce the heat to medium if it looks as though the water may boil over. After 10 minutes, drain and rinse the cashews.

3. Place the cooked cashews, 1 ¼ c. (296 ml) warm water, and all the remaining cashew ricotta cream ingredients in a high-powered blender. Blend until creamy and smooth. Pour into a medium-sized bowl, cover with a plate or plastic wrap, and set aside for now.

4. To prepare the spinach, combine the fresh spinach, olive oil or water, and salt and pepper in a saucepan over medium-high heat and sauté until the spinach is wilted. Set aside for now. Tip: I often do this in the same saucepan I used to boil the cashews to avoid dirtying another pot or pan!

5. Once the squash is cool enough to handle, scoop 3 c. (620 g) of the cooked butternut squash into a clean blender. Add all the remaining butternut squash sauce ingredients and blend until very smooth and creamy. Pour into a separate medium bowl and set aside.

6. Boil the lasagna noodles according to the package directions. Once cooked, carefully lay them out on a clean kitchen towel.

Recipe continues

**FOR BEST GLUTEN FREE VERSION:**
Use gluten free lasagna noodles.

**MAKE-AHEAD TIP:**
This lasagna can be assembled through step 8 as far as 3 days in advance (be sure to save the extra ricotta cream and sage garnish separately so it can be added after baking). Simply cover the unbaked lasagna with plastic wrap before storing in the refrigerator. Take the lasagna out of the fridge to warm to room temperature 1 hour before placing in the oven to bake. Follow the directions in step 9 from there.

7. To assemble the lasagna, spread ¾ c. (177 ml) butternut squash sauce over the bottom of a 9-x-13-inch (23-x-33-cm) baking dish. Place 4 lasagna noodles on top. Spread a heaping ½ c. (119 ml) of ricotta cream sauce over the noodles, then sprinkle half of the spinach on top. Add 1 heaping cup (about 250 ml) butternut squash sauce over the top of the spinach and spread it evenly.

8. Repeat once more, layering the remaining noodles, another heaping ½ c. (119 ml) ricotta cream (you'll have extra for drizzling later), the remaining spinach, and all the remaining butternut squash sauce. Note: You will likely see the spinach through the sauce and that's okay!

9. Cover with foil and bake for 27–30 minutes. Then remove the foil and drizzle the surface with the remaining ricotta cream. Garnish with a few pinches of freshly chopped sage. Allow the lasagna to rest for 7–10 minutes before serving.

**NOTE:**
If your squash is too firm to cut in half, microwave the whole squash for 4–7 minutes to help soften it.

# STUFFED ACORN SQUASH WITH TOASTED PECANS AND POMEGRANATE

*Roasted acorn squash is an incredible-tasting food all on its own, but when it's filled with tangy-sweet pomegranate quinoa that has been tossed with garbanzo beans, bits of chewy dried cranberries, and chopped toasted pecans, it makes for an impressive, crave-worthy main that's pretty enough to be used as a centerpiece.*

## YIELD: 8 SERVINGS

### INGREDIENTS:

- 4 acorn squashes, all roughly equal in size
- 3 Tbsp. (45 ml) olive or avocado oil, divided
- 1 tsp. salt, plus more for squash
- ¼ tsp. black pepper, plus more for squash
- ⅔ c. (80 g) pecans
- 1 ½ c. (356 ml) sweetened pomegranate juice
- 1 Tbsp. (15 ml) maple syrup
- ¾ c. (96 g) chopped yellow or white onion
- 1 ¾ tsp. garlic powder
- 1 ¼ tsp. dried oregano
- 1 ¼ tsp. cumin
- 4 c. (508 g) cooked quinoa, cooled
- 1 c. (153 g) home-cooked or canned garbanzo beans, drained and rinsed
- ½ c. (65 g) dried cranberries, roughly chopped, plus more for topping
- 1 small handful of fresh parsley, chopped

### INSTRUCTIONS:

1. Preheat your oven to 400°F (approx. 204°C).

2. Slice off the stem and pointy bottom on each squash so they can easily stand up on either end. Then, slice horizontally down the center of each one. Scoop out the seeds with a spoon.

3. Using 2 Tbsp. (30 ml) of the oil, liberally brush the insides and top edges of each squash. Lightly sprinkle salt and pepper over the surface of each one.

4. Roast cut side down on a parchment-lined or nonstick baking sheet for 28–30 minutes, or until the skins are very shiny, the flesh is soft, and the top edges of the squash are lightly browned when flipped over.

5. Place the pecans on a separate baking sheet and toast them for just 5 minutes, or until fragrant. Give them a rough chop once cool enough to handle.

6. Meanwhile, heat the pomegranate juice in a small saucepan over medium-high heat. Bring to a boil and maintain that boil for 20–25 minutes, or until juice has reduced by three-quarters, to roughly ¼ c. + 2 Tbsp (97 ml). (Note: Reduce the heat to medium if it seems the juice may boil over.) Remove from the heat and add the maple syrup. Set aside for now.

7. Heat the remaining 1 Tbsp. (15 ml) of oil in a skillet over medium heat for about 30 seconds.

8. Add the onion and sauté until lightly browned, about 2 minutes. Add the garlic powder, oregano, cumin, salt, and pepper and stir until fragrant and onion is evenly coated with spices.

Recipe continues

**FOR BEST GLUTEN FREE VERSION:**
This recipe is naturally gluten free, but check all ingredient labels to be sure.

**MAKE-AHEAD TIP:**
Cook the quinoa up to 3 days in advance and store in the refrigerator. To take it one step further, cook the onion ahead and combine the cooked onion, spices, and quinoa in an airtight container. Store, refrigerated, for up to 3 days. Before serving, heat this mixture in a skillet to warm through, then toss with the pomegranate syrup, garbanzo beans, pecans, and dried cranberries. Note: The pomegranate syrup cannot be made in advance, but you can use store-bought pomegranate molasses in its place.

9. Add the quinoa, garbanzo beans, dried cranberries, ¼ c. (59 ml) of the reduced pomegranate syrup, and half of the chopped pecans to the skillet. Stir until the quinoa is thoroughly coated in pomegranate syrup, about 1 minute.

10. Add a heaping ½ c. (65 g) of quinoa mixture (or however much will fit) to the center of each acorn squash half. Top with the remaining pecans, extra cranberries, and chopped fresh parsley, and drizzle with the remaining pomegranate syrup. Serve immediately.

**NOTES:**
• If your squashes are too firm to cut, microwave them whole for 3–4 minutes to help soften.
• This recipe can also be made with delicata squash, seeded and sliced in half lengthwise, or with a butternut squash, seeded and quartered.

# BAKED MAC AND CHEESE

*Your guests will never suspect that this creamy and super cheesy mac and cheese baked with a crispy breadcrumb topping is free of dairy! Serve it as a main or as a side. Either way, everyone will be back for seconds.*

YIELD: 12 SERVINGS

INGREDIENTS:

Mac and Cheese Base:
- ½ c. (113 g) vegan butter or margarine, plus more for greasing
- ¼ c. + 2 Tbsp. (53 g) all-purpose flour, or ¼ c. + 2 Tbsp. (48 g) tapioca starch
- 3 ½ c. (830 ml) unsweetened, unflavored non-dairy milk, such as almond, cashew, or soy
- ¾ c. (177 ml) low-sodium vegetable broth
- ¼ c. (20 g) nutritional yeast flakes
- 1 vegetable bouillon cube (or 1 tsp. bouillon substitute)
- ½ tsp. paprika
- ¼ tsp. salt, plus more to taste
- ⅛ tsp. black pepper, plus more to taste
- 2 c. (206 g) shredded vegan cheddar cheese, plus more to taste
- 16 oz. (454 g) elbow macaroni noodles

Topping:
- ¾ c. (68 g) panko breadcrumbs
- 3 Tbsp. (15 g) nutritional yeast flakes
- 1 tsp. onion powder
- ½ tsp. garlic powder
- ½ tsp. salt
- ¼ tsp. black pepper
- ¼ c. (56 g) vegan butter or margarine, melted

FOR BEST GLUTEN FREE VERSION:
Use the tapioca starch option instead of the regular all-purpose flour, and use gluten free elbow macaroni noodles. Use gluten free breadcrumbs (the panko type, if possible), for the topping.

INSTRUCTIONS:

1. Melt the butter in a 3-quart or larger saucepan over medium-high heat. Add the flour or starch and whisk until all flour is incorporated.

2. Add the non-dairy milk and broth and whisk until it becomes bubbly. Continue whisking as it boils until the mixture starts to thicken, about 5 minutes. Keep in mind, it will thicken quite a bit more after all the remaining ingredients are added.

3. Remove the pan from the heat and add the nutritional yeast flakes, vegetable bouillon, paprika, salt, and pepper and stir well. Once combined, whisk in the vegan cheese. Note: You may need to place the pan back over low heat for the cheese to completely melt. It may take several minutes of whisking to become smooth.

4. Carefully taste and add more cheese for a cheesier flavor, and add salt and pepper to taste. Cover and set sauce aside for now.

5. Preheat your oven to 350°F (approx. 177°C). Grease a 9-x-13-in. (23-x-33-cm) or other 3-quart baking dish with butter and set aside for now.

6. Cook the elbow pasta in boiling water according to the package directions. Drain well and add the pasta to the pot containing the sauce. Stir well to coat all the macaroni noodles. Add salt to taste.

7. Pour the mac and cheese into the prepared baking dish and smooth over the surface.

8. In a small bowl, stir together the first six ingredients for the topping. Add the melted butter and stir again. Sprinkle this mixture evenly over the surface of the mac and cheese.

9. Bake for 25–30 minutes, or until lightly golden brown around the edges. Let the mac and cheese rest 5 minutes before serving.

NOTE:
If sensitive to salt, use low-sodium vegetable bouillon cubes. You can always add more salt to taste afterward.

MAKE-AHEAD TIP:
Assemble the mac and cheese base 1 day prior to serving by following steps 1 through 7. Let it cool for 15 minutes before covering with plastic wrap and placing in the fridge overnight. The next day, remove the dish from the refrigerator and allow it to warm to room temperature for 1 hour. Add the topping and bake according to steps 8 and 9.

# SHEPHERD'S PIE

*This hearty shepherd's pie is true comfort food, offering the familiar flavors of tomato, garlic, loads of veggies, and creamy mashed potatoes. Serve it on Thanksgiving or anytime during the holiday weekend to satisfy both the tastebuds and bellies of your hungry family and friends.*

YIELD: 8–10 SERVINGS

INGREDIENTS:
- 1 batch Classic Mashed Potatoes (page 46)
- 1 Tbsp. (14 g) vegan butter or margarine, plus more for greasing
- 1 c. (128 g) chopped yellow or white onion
- 1 c. (140 g) chopped carrots (peeling is optional)
- ½ c. (60 g) diced celery
- ⅔ c. (75 g) frozen or fresh corn
- ⅔ c. (93 g) frozen or fresh peas
- 2 medium cloves garlic, minced
- ¼ c. (35 g) all-purpose flour
- 3 Tbsp. (45 g) tomato paste
- 2 ½ tsp. finely chopped fresh thyme (or ¾ tsp. dried thyme)
- 2 ½ tsp. finely chopped fresh sage (or ¾ tsp. dried sage)
- 1 tsp. salt, plus more to taste
- ¼ tsp. black pepper, plus more to taste
- 1 (15-oz. / 425-g) can lentils, drained and rinsed
- 3 c. (711 ml) low-sodium vegetable broth
- ¼ c. (59 ml) red wine
- Chopped fresh parsley for garnish

FOR BEST GLUTEN FREE VERSION:
Simply use gluten free all-purpose flour in place of the regular all-purpose flour.

INSTRUCTIONS:
1. Prepare the mashed potatoes according to the recipe on page 46, then cover with a lid or plastic wrap and set aside until they're needed.
2. Preheat your oven to 400°F (approx. 204°C). Grease a 9-x-13-inch (23-x-33-cm) or other 3-quart baking dish with butter. Set aside for now.
3. Melt the butter in a large skillet or pot over medium-high heat. Add the onion, carrots, and celery and sauté until slightly soft, 3–5 minutes.
4. Add the corn, peas, garlic, flour, tomato paste, thyme, sage, salt, and pepper and stir until vegetables are evenly coated and the peas and corn are warmed through, about 1 minute.
5. Stir in the lentils, broth, and wine and bring the mixture to a rapid simmer. Continue cooking, stirring occasionally, until the mixture starts to thicken, about 10 minutes.
6. Transfer the lentil mixture to your prepared 3-quart dish and smooth over the surface.
7. Top the lentil mixture with mashed potatoes a little at a time. Note: If your mashed potatoes have dried out a bit, mash in an extra splash or two of non-dairy milk before adding to the casserole dish. Completely smooth over the surface of the potatoes, or leave some peaks and valleys for a more rustic design. If you're feeling fancy, add a thin layer of mashed potatoes first, then transfer the remaining potatoes to a piping bag with a large star tip and pipe the remaining potatoes over the surface.
8. Bake for 20 minutes or until the edges start to bubble and brown. Allow the shepherd's pie to rest 5–10 minutes before serving. Garnish with fresh chopped parsley.

MAKE-AHEAD TIP:
This shepherd's pie can be assembled as far as 3 days in advance. Simply follow steps 1–7, then cover in plastic wrap before storing in the refrigerator. Take the pie out of the fridge to warm to room temperature 1 hour before placing in the oven.

# BAKED BEAN CORNBREAD CASSEROLE

*Honestly, you can't go wrong with savory-sweet baked beans topped with a glorious golden layer of cornbread. It's so darn good and so simple to make.*

YIELD: 8 SERVINGS

INGREDIENTS:

**Baked Bean Layer:**
- 1 Tbsp. (15 ml) neutral-flavored oil, plus more for greasing
- ⅔ c. (85 g) chopped white or yellow onion
- ½ c. (70 g) chopped green bell pepper
- 30 oz. (850 g) canned baked beans
- ⅓ c. (60 g) tomato paste
- ⅓ c. (79 ml) water
- ¼ tsp. black pepper
- Salt to taste

**Cornbread Layer:**
- 1 ½ c. (356 g) unsweetened unflavored non-dairy milk, such as almond, cashew, or soy
- 1 Tbsp. (15 ml) white distilled vinegar
- 1 ¼ c. (196 g) cornmeal
- ¾ c. (105 g) all-purpose flour
- 1 Tbsp. + 1 tsp. (16 g) baking powder
- 1 tsp. salt
- ¼ c. (59 ml) neutral-flavored oil
- 3 Tbsp. (45 ml) maple syrup
- ½ c. (56 g) fresh or thawed frozen corn
- ½ c. (60 g) shredded vegan cheddar cheese

**FOR BEST GLUTEN FREE VERSION:**
Use gluten free all-purpose flour in the cornbread layer and add ½ tsp. xanthan gum to the dry mixture in step 5 if your flour mix doesn't already contain it. Check all remaining ingredient labels to ensure they're gluten free as well.

INSTRUCTIONS:

1. Preheat your oven to 400°F (approx. 204°C). Grease a 7-x-11-inch (18-x-28-cm) or other 2-quart dish with oil. Set aside.
2. For the baked bean layer, start by heating the oil in a large skillet over medium-high heat for about 30 seconds. Add the onion and bell pepper and cook until lightly browned, 4–5 minutes. Turn off the heat.
3. Add the baked beans, tomato paste, water, and black pepper to the skillet and stir to combine. Give the mixture a taste and add a pinch of salt, if needed. (Mine usually doesn't need it, but salt levels vary with canned baked beans.) Cover the skillet and set aside for now.
4. For the cornbread, combine the milk and vinegar in a small bowl and stir well to mix. (It will curdle, and that's what you want!) Set aside.
5. In a medium mixing bowl, combine the cornmeal, flour, baking powder, and salt and whisk together.
6. Add the oil, maple syrup, and milk mixture to the mixing bowl and whisk until smooth with no clumps. Fold in the corn. Allow the batter to rest for 5 minutes.
7. Pour the baked bean mixture into your prepared dish and smooth over the surface.
8. Slowly pour the cornbread batter over the baked beans and spread evenly to create a second layer.
9. Bake for 25 minutes, then remove from the oven and sprinkle the shredded cheese evenly over the surface. Quickly return to the oven for an additional 15–18 minutes, or until the edges are golden brown and the center feels firm to the touch. Let rest for 10 minutes before serving.

**MAKE-AHEAD TIP:**
The baked bean layer (steps 2 and 3) can be made up to 2 days in advance. Allow the mixture to cool for 15 minutes before storing in an airtight container in the fridge. When needed, allow baked beans to warm to room temperature for 30 minutes before transferring to the baking dish. Note: If the baked beans have become very thick, stir in a tablespoon or two of water before transferring to the baking dish.

# CHEESY LOADED ROASTED CAULIFLOWER CASSEROLE

*This crazy-delicious cheesy cauliflower casserole was almost placed in the "sides" category of this book, but ultimately I felt it was just too grand and special and stick-to-your-ribs satisfying to not make it as a "main." Switch things up this Thanksgiving and give this casserole a try!*

YIELD: 12 SERVINGS

INGREDIENTS:
- 2 ½–3 lb. (1135–1360 g) bite-sized cauliflower florets (from about 2 medium heads)
- 2 Tbsp. (30 ml) olive oil
- 1 ¼ tsp. salt, divided
- ½ tsp. black pepper, divided
- 2 c. (240 g) shredded vegan cheddar cheese, divided
- ¾ c. (169 g) vegan cream cheese, softened to room temperature
- ¾ c. (about 155 g) vegan unsweetened plain yogurt or vegan sour cream
- ½ tsp. garlic powder
- ⅓ c. (31 g) panko breadcrumbs
- 3 Tbsp. (42 g) vegan butter or margarine, melted
- 5 strips vegan bacon
- 3 scallions, white and light green parts only, thinly sliced

FOR BEST GLUTEN FREE VERSION:
Use gluten free breadcrumbs (the panko type, if possible). Check to make sure your bacon is gluten free as well.

INSTRUCTIONS:
1. Preheat your oven to 425°F (approx. 218°C).
2. Place the cauliflower florets in a 3-quart baking dish. Toss with the olive oil, 1 tsp. salt, and ¼ tsp. black pepper. Roast for 30 minutes.
3. Meanwhile, mix together 1 c. (120 g) of the shredded cheese, the cream cheese, yogurt or sour cream, garlic powder, and the remaining ¼ tsp. salt and ¼ tsp. black pepper until well combined. Dollop the surface of the cauliflower with this mixture just after removing it from the oven, and carefully spread so the creamy mixture reaches all sides and corners of the pan.
4. Sprinkle the remaining 1 c. (120 g) shredded cheese across the surface, followed by the breadcrumbs, then drizzle the melted butter over the top.
5. Bake for 15–20 minutes, or until the cheese is melted and parts of the surface are slightly browned. Place under the broiler for a few seconds, if needed for more browning.
6. Meanwhile, cook the bacon in a skillet until browned on both sides. If it seems overly dry, spray or brush the bacon with a light coating of oil. Once cool enough to handle, chop into small pieces or strips.
7. When the casserole is done baking, sprinkle the surface with bacon and scallions. Serve immediately.

MAKE-AHEAD TIP:
Chop the cauliflower up to 1 day in advance and store in an airtight container or resealable plastic bag in the fridge until needed. You can also mix together the cream cheese mixture (as described in step 3) in advance and store it in an airtight container in the fridge for up to 3 days.

# SIDES

# SWEET POTATO CASSEROLE WITH BROWN SUGAR AND PECANS

*How do you make sweetened, buttery sweet potatoes taste even better? You top them with a mixture starring brown sugar and crunchy pecans, that's how! This sweet potato casserole will knock your socks off, and that's all there is to it.*

### YIELD: ABOUT 12 SERVINGS

### INGREDIENTS:
- 4 lb. (1776 g) yams or other orange-colored sweet potatoes (you'll need 8 c. cooked sweet potato)
- 1 c. (230 g) granulated sugar
- ⅔ c. (151 g) vegan butter or margarine, softened, plus more for greasing
- ½ c. (119 ml) unsweetened, unflavored non-dairy milk
- 2 tsp. vanilla extract
- 1 tsp. salt

### Brown Sugar and Pecan Topping:
- ¾ c. (162 g) light brown sugar, packed
- ⅔ c. (93 g) all-purpose flour
- ⅓ c. + 1 Tbsp. (85 g) cold vegan butter or margarine, cut into ½-inch (1.25-cm) cubes
- 1 c. (120 g) pecans, chopped

### FOR BEST GLUTEN FREE VERSION:
Simply replace the all-purpose flour with gluten free all-purpose flour. Check all remaining labels to ensure they're gluten free as well.

### MAKE-AHEAD TIP:
This dish can be assembled through step 5 and then covered in plastic wrap and stored in the refrigerator for up to 2 days. The day you need it, allow the casserole to sit on the counter at room temperature for 1 hour before following steps 6–8.

### INSTRUCTIONS:
1. Preheat your oven to 375°F (approx. 190°C). Pierce each potato 3–4 times with a fork. Bake on a parchment-lined or nonstick baking sheet until juice oozes from the potatoes and they're very soft. This could take anywhere from 45–90 minutes, depending on the size of the potatoes.
2. After removing the potatoes from the oven, reduce the heat to 350°F (approx. 177°C) and grease a 3-quart baking dish, such as a 9-x-13-inch (approx. 23-x-33-cm) dish, with butter. Set aside for now.
3. Once the potatoes are cool enough to handle, scoop the cooked flesh out of the potato skins and into a large mixing bowl (you should have about 8 c. worth). Add the sugar, butter, milk, vanilla, and salt to the bowl.
4. Using a handheld mixer, mix on medium-high speed until smooth, about 1 minute. Alternatively, you can use a stand mixer or potato masher.
5. Transfer the potato mixture to your prepared baking dish and smooth over the surface.
6. To make the topping, stir together the brown sugar and flour in a medium-sized mixing bowl, breaking up any clumps as you go. Add the cubed butter and work it into the mixture with your hands or a pastry cutter until crumbly. Add the pecans and stir to combine.
7. Sprinkle the topping evenly over the surface of the sweet potatoes.
8. Bake for 30–35 minutes, or until pecans appear medium brown and toasted. Let the casserole rest for 10 minutes before serving. This dish is great served hot or slightly warm.

# CLASSIC MASHED POTATOES

*Rarely do you see a Thanksgiving spread that doesn't include a big batch of classic mashed potatoes. I'm happy to say that this recipe presents a simple method for making perfect, crowd-pleasing mashed potatoes each and every time. Be sure to check out the Make-Ahead Tip below to see how to save yourself loads of time on Thanksgiving Day.*

YIELD: 6–8 SERVINGS

INGREDIENTS:

- 3 lb. (1361 g) russet potatoes, peeled and chopped into 2-inch (5-cm) pieces
- ½ c. + 1 Tbsp. (133 ml) unsweetened, unflavored non-dairy milk, such as almond, cashew, or soy, plus more as needed
- ⅓ c. + 1 Tbsp. (85 g) vegan butter or margarine
- 1 ½ tsp. salt, plus more to taste
- ¼ tsp. black pepper, plus more to taste (I usually add an extra ⅛ tsp.)
- A couple pinches of chopped fresh parsley for garnish (optional)

FOR BEST GLUTEN FREE VERSION:
This recipe is naturally gluten free, but check all ingredient labels to be sure.

MAKE-AHEAD TIP:
The potatoes can be peeled, chopped, and stored completely covered in water in an airtight container in the fridge for 3–4 days before using. When ready to cook, allow the potatoes to sit at room temperature for 30–60 minutes before placing in the pot with fresh water to boil.

INSTRUCTIONS:

1. Place the potatoes in a pot and cover with water. Set over medium-high heat and bring the water to a boil. Meanwhile, measure out the milk and butter and set aside so that they're not overly cold when added to the potatoes.

2. Continue boiling the potatoes until they are very fork-tender, 10–12 minutes.

3. Drain potatoes well and return them to the pot.

4. Add the milk, butter, salt, and pepper and mash thoroughly with a potato masher until potatoes are smooth yet fluffy. Alternatively, you can use an electric handheld mixer to do the job.

5. For creamier mashed potatoes, add an extra splash or two of milk. Add extra salt and pepper to taste.

6. Immediately cover the potatoes with a lid or plastic wrap until ready to serve. I usually mash in an extra tablespoon or two of milk just before transferring to a bowl to serve as they tend to dry out slightly as they sit. Garnish with chopped fresh parsley before serving, if desired.

# GARLIC RED SKINNED MASHED POTATOES

*For mashed potatoes that offer a bit more garlicky goodness and texture, look no further. These garlic red-skinned mashed potatoes are a fun yet subtle way to mix things up on Thanksgiving. Best of all: no peeling required.*

YIELD: ABOUT 10 SERVINGS

INGREDIENTS:

- 3 lb. (1360 g) red potatoes, scrubbed and chopped into 2-inch (5-cm) chunks (do not peel)
- 4 medium cloves garlic, peeled
- ¾ c. (177 ml) unsweetened, unflavored non-dairy milk, such as almond, cashew, or soy, plus more as needed
- ½ c. (113 g) vegan butter or margarine
- ⅓ c. (about 68 g) vegan sour cream
- 1 ¼ tsp. salt, plus more to taste
- ¼ tsp. black pepper, plus more to taste

FOR BEST GLUTEN FREE VERSION:
This recipe is naturally gluten free, but check all ingredient labels to be sure.

MAKE-AHEAD TIP:
The potatoes can be chopped and stored completely covered in water in an airtight container in the fridge for 3–4 days before using. When ready to cook, allow the potatoes to sit at room temperature for 30–60 minutes before placing in a pot with fresh water to boil.

INSTRUCTIONS:

1. Rinse the chopped potatoes thoroughly until the water runs clear.
2. Place the potatoes and peeled garlic cloves in a large pot and fill with enough water to cover the potatoes.
3. Bring the water to a boil. Continue cooking until the potatoes are very fork-tender. Meanwhile, measure out the milk, butter and sour cream and set aside so that they're not overly cold when added to the potatoes.
4. Drain the potatoes and garlic well, then return them to the pot and turn the heat to medium-low for about a minute to help remove any excess water.
5. Add ½ c. (119 ml) milk, the butter, sour cream, salt, and pepper and mash well. Add the remaining ¼ c. (58 ml) milk and mash again. For creamier mashed potatoes, add more milk, one splash at a time, until the desired consistency is reached. Cover the pot with a lid or plastic wrap until just before serving.

# MOM'S SWEET POTATOES WITH MARSHMALLOWS

*Thanksgiving in our house wouldn't feel complete if my mom didn't make her awesome candied sweet potatoes topped with marshmallows. This recipe has been a family favorite for years. The only bad part is that there are rarely any leftovers at the end of the feast to enjoy the next day!*

YIELD: 8 SERVINGS

INGREDIENTS:
- 2 lb. (888 g) yams or other orange-colored sweet potatoes (you'll need 4 c. cooked sweet potato)
- ½ c. + 2 Tbsp. (144 g) granulated sugar
- ⅓ c. (75 g) vegan butter or margarine, softened, plus more for greasing
- ¼ c. (59 ml) bourbon or orange juice
- 1 tsp. vanilla extract
- 1 tsp. salt
- 1 ½ c. (134 g) mini vegan marshmallows

FOR BEST GLUTEN FREE VERSION:
This recipe is naturally gluten free, but check all ingredient labels to be sure.

MAKE-AHEAD TIP:
This dish can be assembled as far as 3 days in advance, but hold off on topping with marshmallows until just before baking. Simply prepare the potatoes through step 5, then cover in plastic wrap before storing in the refrigerator. Take the dish out of the fridge to warm to room temperature 1 hour before adding the marshmallows and placing in the oven.

INSTRUCTIONS:
1. Preheat your oven to 375°F (approx. 190°C). Pierce each sweet potato 3–4 times with a fork. Bake on a parchment-lined or nonstick baking sheet until juice oozes from the potatoes and they're very soft. This could take anywhere from 45–90 minutes, depending on the size of the potatoes.
2. After removing the potatoes from the oven, reduce the heat to 350°F (approx. 177°C). Grease the sides and bottom of a 2-quart dish, such as a 7-x-11-inch (18-x-28-cm) baking dish, with butter. Set aside for now.
3. Once the potatoes are cool enough to handle, scoop the cooked flesh out of the potato skins and into a mixing bowl (you should have about 4 c. worth). Add the sugar, butter, bourbon or juice, vanilla, and salt to the bowl.
4. Using a handheld mixer, mix on medium-high speed until very smooth, about 1 minute. Alternatively, you can use a stand mixer or potato masher.
5. Transfer the potato mixture to your prepared dish and smooth over the surface.
6. Sprinkle the mini marshmallows evenly over the top and bake for 25–30 minutes. For lightly browned marshmallows, you may need to place the dish under a broiler for a few seconds. Alternatively, you can use a kitchen torch.
7. Allow the sweet potatoes to rest at room temperature for 5 minutes before serving.

# CORNBREAD STUFFING

*For those who hold a special place in their hearts for cornbread, this stuffing recipe is a must! The comforting flavor of lightly sweetened cornbread is truly the star in this dish, with the savory flavors of sage, thyme, and onion complementing it beautifully. This is also the ideal stuffing for those avoiding gluten, since it's simple to make a gluten free version of the Sweet Cornbread recipe.*

YIELD: 8 SERVINGS

INGREDIENTS:

- 1 batch Sweet Cornbread (page 85), baked and cooled
- ¾ c. (170 g) vegan butter or margarine, plus more for greasing
- 2 c. (256 g) chopped yellow onion
- ¾ c. (90 g) chopped celery
- 3 Tbsp. (6 g) finely chopped fresh sage (or 3 tsp. dried sage)
- 2 Tbsp. (5 g) finely chopped fresh thyme (or 2 tsp. dried thyme)
- 2 Tbsp. (4 g) finely chopped fresh parsley (or 2 tsp. dried parsley)
- 1 tsp. finely chopped fresh rosemary (or heaping ¼ tsp. dried rosemary)
- ¾ tsp. salt, plus more to taste
- ½ tsp. black pepper, plus more to taste
- 1 c. (237 ml) low-sodium vegetable broth
- ¾ c. (177 ml) unsweetened, unflavored non-dairy milk

FOR BEST GLUTEN FREE VERSION:
Use the gluten free version when preparing the sweet cornbread.

MAKE-AHEAD TIP:
This stuffing can be completely assembled (but not baked) as far as 3 days in advance. Simply cover in plastic wrap before storing in the refrigerator. Take the stuffing out of the fridge to warm to room temperature 1 hour before placing in the oven to bake.

INSTRUCTIONS:

1. Once the Sweet Cornbread is completely cooled, preheat your oven to 375°F (approx. 190°C). Slide a knife around the edges of the cornbread to help loosen it, then turn the cornbread out onto a flat working surface. Cut cornbread into ½–1-inch (1.25–2.5-cm) cubes. Transfer to a parchment-lined or nonstick baking sheet and toast in the oven for 20 minutes. In the end, you should have 8 ½–9 c. cornbread cubes. Allow to cool completely.

2. After the cubes have cooled, preheat your oven once again to 375°F (approx. 190°C). Grease a 2-quart dish such as a 7-x-11-inch (18-x-28-cm) baking dish with butter (see note below).

3. Melt the butter in a large skillet over medium-high heat. Add the onions and celery and cook, stirring occasionally, until soft and translucent, 8–10 minutes.

4. Turn off the heat and stir in the herbs, salt, and pepper, then stir in the broth and milk.

5. Transfer the cornbread cubes to a large bowl. Ladle the onion and celery mixture over the bread until you can easily pick up the skillet and pour the remaining mixture into the bowl.

6. Using a long-handled spoon or spatula, gently fold to evenly coat the bread cubes, but do not overmix. Taste a cube or two and add an extra pinch of salt and pepper if needed.

7. Transfer the stuffing mixture to your prepared dish and gently spread until it reaches all corners and edges.

8. Bake for 35 minutes, or until the top is lightly crispy.

NOTE:
For crispier stuffing, bake in a 3-quart dish such as a 9-x-13-inch (23-x-33-cm) dish instead. I actually love it made this way.

# CLASSIC HERB STUFFING

*In my opinion, a good Thanksgiving stuffing needs to have a good balance of onions and celery. It needs to be loaded with festive herbs of the season, and it absolutely must have the right amount of moisture coming from melted butter and broth. This is my version of "perfect" classic herb stuffing. I hope you love it, too.*

YIELD: 8 SERVINGS

INGREDIENTS:

- 1 medium loaf French, ciabatta, or other white bread
- ½ c. (113 g) vegan butter or margarine, plus more for greasing
- 1 c. (128 g) chopped yellow onion
- 1 c. (120 g) chopped celery
- 2 Tbsp. (4 g) finely chopped fresh sage (or 2 tsp. dried sage)
- 1 Tbsp. (4 g) finely chopped fresh rosemary (or 1 tsp. dried rosemary)
- 1 Tbsp. (2 g) finely chopped fresh basil (or 1 tsp. dried basil)
- ½ Tbsp. finely chopped fresh thyme (or ½ tsp. dried thyme)
- ½ tsp. salt, plus more to taste
- ¼ tsp. black pepper, plus more to taste
- 2 ¾ c. (650 ml) low-sodium vegetable broth, divided, plus more as needed

FOR BEST GLUTEN FREE VERSION:
Try this recipe with store-bought gluten free stuffing cubes or your favorite loaf of gluten free bread.

MAKE-AHEAD TIP:
This stuffing can be completely assembled (but not baked) as far as 3 days in advance. Simply cover in plastic wrap before storing in the refrigerator. Take the stuffing out of the fridge to warm to room temperature 1 hour before placing in the oven to bake.

INSTRUCTIONS:

1. Chop the bread into 1-inch (2.5-cm) cubes (you should have about 7 c. bread cubes in all) and spread them evenly on a baking sheet or two. Allow the bread to dry out uncovered at room temperature for 2–3 days, or until dry and crunchy. Alternatively, you can toast the freshly chopped bread cubes in a 375°F (approx. 190°C) oven for 10–12 minutes, or until dry.

2. Preheat your oven to 350°F (approx. 177°C).

3. Grease a 2-quart dish such as a 7-x-11-inch (18-x-28-cm) baking dish with butter. Set aside.

4. Melt the butter in a large skillet over medium-high heat. Add the onion and celery and cook until slightly soft, about 5 minutes.

5. Add the herbs, salt, and pepper and stir to combine.

6. Slowly pour 2 c. (474 ml) of broth into the mixture and then turn off the heat.

7. Place the dried bread cubes in a large mixing bowl. Ladle the herb and broth mixture over the top. When it gets to the point that you're able, pick up the skillet and pour the broth mixture into the bowl instead.

8. Using a long-handled spoon or spatula, toss the bread until it is evenly coated with broth and herbs. Sample a piece or two and add more salt and pepper if needed.

9. Transfer the stuffing mixture one heaping spoonful at a time into your prepared dish. Pour the remaining ¾ c. (178 ml) broth evenly over the surface.

10. Bake for 25 minutes or until the tips of any bread cubes sticking up are golden and slightly crispy. Serve immediately.

NOTE:
For super moist stuffing, add an extra ½ c. (237 ml) heated broth over the surface of the stuffing just before serving.

# SAUSAGE APPLE STUFFING

*As much as we all love it, it's easy to take stuffing for granted on Thanksgiving. It's always served, and typically with very little variation from year to year. That is, until now. This sausage apple stuffing is insanely good. I dare you to make it and say that it's not your new favorite stuffing recipe! (Be sure to check out my note on how to find a good vegan sausage.)*

YIELD: 8 SERVINGS

INGREDIENTS:
- 1 small to medium-sized loaf French, ciabatta, or other white bread
- 8 oz. (about 227 g) vegan breakfast sausage patties
- ⅓ c. + 1 Tbsp. (85 g) vegan butter or margarine, plus more for greasing
- 1 c. (128 g) chopped yellow onion
- ¾ c. (90 g) chopped celery
- 1 unpeeled Granny Smith apple (or other apple of choice), cored and diced
- 2 tsp. dried sage
- ½ tsp. dried thyme
- 1 small handful of fresh parsley, chopped
- ½ tsp. salt, plus more to taste
- ¼ tsp. black pepper, plus more to taste
- 1 c. (237 ml) low-sodium vegetable broth
- ¾ c. (97 g) dried cranberries

FOR BEST GLUTEN FREE VERSION:
Try this recipe with store-bought gluten free stuffing cubes or your favorite loaf of gluten free bread. Check all remaining ingredient labels to ensure they're gluten free as well.

MAKE-AHEAD TIP:
This stuffing can be completely assembled (but not baked) as far as 3 days in advance. Simply cover in plastic wrap before storing in the refrigerator. Take the stuffing out of the fridge to warm to room temperature 1 hour before placing in the oven to bake.

INSTRUCTIONS:
1. Chop the bread into 1-inch (2.5-cm) cubes (you should have about 6 c. bread cubes in all) and spread them evenly on a baking sheet or two. Allow the bread to dry out uncovered at room temperature for 2–3 days, or until dry and crunchy. Alternatively, you can place the freshly chopped bread cubes in a 375°F (approx. 190°C) oven for 10–12 minutes, or until dry.
2. Preheat your oven to 375°F (approx. 190°C). Grease a 2-quart dish such as a 7-x-11-inch (18-x-28-cm) baking dish with butter. Set aside.
3. In a large skillet, cook the breakfast sausage until browned on both sides. Transfer to a cutting board and, once cool enough to handle, chop into ½-inch (1.5-cm) pieces. Set aside for now.
4. In the same skillet, melt the butter over medium-high heat. Add the onions, celery, and apple and cook for 4–5 minutes, until slightly soft. Turn off the heat and stir in the sage, thyme, parsley, salt, and pepper.
5. In a large bowl, combine the bread cubes, chopped sausage, onion-butter mixture, vegetable broth, and dried cranberries. Toss together until well combined. Take a bite or two to check the seasoning and add more salt and pepper if needed.
6. Transfer the stuffing to the prepared baking dish, and press down slightly. Bake for 25–30 minutes, or until crispy on top.

NOTE:
I feel soy-based vegan breakfast sausage has the best texture and flavor.

# BALSAMIC-GLAZED BRUSSELS SPROUTS

*Our family has hardly met a roasted Brussels sprouts recipe that we didn't love, but this one is truly our favorite. It's simple to make and absolutely bursting with flavor thanks to the addition of balsamic glaze.*

YIELD: 4–6 SERVINGS

INGREDIENTS:
- 6 c. (540 g) trimmed and halved Brussels sprouts
- 1 Tbsp. (15 ml) olive oil or avocado oil
- ½ tsp. garlic powder (optional)
- Scant ½ tsp. salt, plus more to taste
- ¼ tsp. black pepper, plus more to taste
- 4 strips vegan bacon (optional)
- ¼ c. (59 ml) balsamic glaze or syrupy aged balsamic

FOR BEST GLUTEN FREE VERSION:
This recipe is naturally gluten free, but check all ingredient labels to be sure.

MAKE-AHEAD TIP:
Trim and slice the Brussels sprouts up to 3 days in advance. Store in an airtight container or resealable storage bag in the fridge until needed.

INSTRUCTIONS:
1. Preheat your oven to 400°F (approx. 204°C).
2. Place the Brussels sprouts in a mixing bowl and toss with the oil. Add the garlic powder, if using, along with the salt and pepper, and toss again. Tip: No need to wash your bowl right away—you'll be using it again after the Brussels sprouts have roasted!
3. Spread the sprouts evenly on a parchment-lined or nonstick baking sheet (or two), cut side down.
4. Roast for 15 minutes. Remove the sprouts from the oven to flip, then reduce your oven temperature to 350°F (approx. 177°C). Immediately return the Brussels sprouts to the oven for an additional 15–20 minutes or until brown and crispy.
5. Meanwhile, cook the bacon in a skillet until browned on both sides, if using. If your bacon seems overly dry, coat each side lightly with oil. Once cool enough to handle, chop or slice it into small pieces.
6. Transfer your roasted sprouts back to the mixing bowl and toss with the chopped bacon and balsamic glaze to evenly coat. Taste and add more salt and pepper as needed. Spoon the Brussels sprouts onto your serving dish of choice and serve immediately.

# ROASTED ROOT VEGETABLES WITH APPLE CIDER GLAZE

*Your Thanksgiving plate will be elevated to a new level of deliciousness after adding these colorful roasted root vegetables with apple cider glaze. The flavor of the apple cider really shines through and is the perfect match for these tender and lightly browned autumn veggies.*

YIELD: 8–10 SERVINGS

INGREDIENTS:

- 1 (2-lb. / 907-g) butternut squash, peeled, seeded, and chopped into ½–1-inch (approx. 1.5–2.5-cm) cubes
- 1 lb. (454 g) parsnips, peeled and sliced into ¼-inch (approx. 0.5-cm)-thick coins
- 1 lb. (454 g) carrots, peeled and chopped into ¼–inch (approx. 0.5–cm)-thick coins
- 1 lb. (454 g) turnips, peeled and chopped into ½–1-inch (approx. 1.5–2.5-cm) cubes
- 3 Tbsp. (45 ml) olive oil
- 1 Tbsp. (2.5 g) chopped fresh thyme (or 1 tsp. dried thyme)
- 1 Tbsp. (4 g) chopped fresh rosemary (or 1 tsp. dried rosemary)
- 1 ¼ tsp. salt
- ¼ tsp. black pepper
- 3 c. (711 ml) apple cider or all-natural apple juice
- ¼ c. (59 ml) apple cider vinegar
- 1 Tbsp. (14 g) granulated sugar

FOR BEST GLUTEN FREE VERSION:
This recipe is naturally gluten free, but check all ingredient labels to be sure.

INSTRUCTIONS:

1.  Preheat your oven to 425°F (approx. 218°C).
2.  In a large bowl, toss together the squash, parsnips, carrots, turnips, and oil.
3.  Add the thyme, rosemary, salt, and pepper and mix well to coat the vegetables.
4.  Spread the vegetables onto two parchment-lined or nonstick baking sheets in single layers. Roast for 35–40 minutes or until tender and browned, flipping at the 20-minute mark. (Don't wash your bowl just yet! You'll use it again).
5.  Meanwhile, combine the apple cider, apple cider vinegar, and sugar in a medium saucepan and bring to a boil over high heat. Once boiling, lower the heat to medium-high and continue stirring occasionally until reduced to ⅓ c. (79 ml), about 30 minutes.
6.  Transfer the roasted vegetables back to the large bowl and carefully toss with the hot apple cider glaze. Serve immediately.

MAKE-AHEAD TIP:
Peel and chop or slice all the vegetables up to 3 days in advance and store in an airtight container or resealable storage bag. For the cider glaze, combine the ingredients in a large mason jar or other container (but do not cook) up to 3 days in advance so the mixture is ready to go.

# GREEN BEAN CASSEROLE

*This green bean casserole recipe is simply a "veganized" version of the original; tender green beans mixed with a delectable creamed mushroom base and topped with those addictive, oh-so-salty crispy fried onions. If you loved the original version, I'm betting you'll love this one, too.*

YIELD: ABOUT 12 SERVINGS

INGREDIENTS:

- 3 ¼ tsp. salt, divided, plus more to taste
- 2 lb. (907 g) green beans, trimmed and chopped into roughly 1 ½-inch (about 4-cm) pieces
- 2 Tbsp. (30 ml) olive oil or avocado oil, plus more for greasing
- 3 c. (170 g) white mushrooms, sliced into ½-inch (about 1.5-cm) slices
- 4 medium cloves garlic, minced
- ¼ c. (35 g) all-purpose flour, or ¼ c. (37 g) garbanzo bean (chickpea) flour
- 1 c. (237 ml) low-sodium vegetable broth
- 1 ½ c. (356 ml) unsweetened, unflavored non-dairy milk, such as almond, cashew, or soy
- ½ c. (119 ml) canned full-fat coconut milk (shake well before opening and stir well before measuring)
- ½ tsp. black pepper, plus more to taste
- ½ tsp. onion powder
- 6 oz. (174 g) French fried onions, divided

FOR BEST GLUTEN FREE VERSION:
Use the garbanzo bean flour option instead of the all-purpose flour, and use gluten free French fried onions.

INSTRUCTIONS:

1. Fill a 4-quart or larger pot three-quarters of the way with water and add 2 tsp. of the salt. Bring the salted water to a boil, then add the prepared green beans. Boil for 4–5 minutes, or until the green beans are bright green and tender. Drain and set aside for now.

2. Meanwhile, preheat your oven to 400°F (approx. 204°C). Grease a 3-quart dish, such as a 9-x-13-inch (23-x-33-cm) baking dish, with oil and set aside.

3. Heat the oil in a large skillet over medium heat for about 30 seconds. Add the mushrooms and garlic and sauté until soft, 3–5 minutes.

4. Sprinkle the flour over the surface and stir to coat the mushrooms. Slowly add the vegetable broth and stir until the mixture thickens.

5. Add the milk, coconut milk, remaining 1 ¼ tsp. salt, the pepper, and onion powder and cook, stirring occasionally, until thickened, 4–5 minutes. Remove the skillet from the heat.

6. Add the cooked green beans and ½ c. (32 g) of the French fried onions to the skillet. Stir to combine. Give the mixture a taste and add more salt and pepper, if needed.

7. Transfer the green bean mixture to your prepared dish and spread evenly.

8. Sprinkle the remaining French fried onions evenly over the surface.

9. Bake for 15–20 minutes, or until piping hot and the onions are lightly browned. Serve immediately.

MAKE-AHEAD TIP:
This recipe can be assembled through step 7 up to 2 days in advance and stored covered in plastic wrap in the refrigerator. When ready for it, allow the dish to sit at room temperature for 1 hour before topping with the remaining French fried onions and placing in the oven to bake.

# CREAMED CORN

*Don't underestimate this recipe… it may sound simple and somewhat forgettable, but I assure you, it's the complete opposite! The ingredients in this creamed corn come together wonderfully to create a side dish so good, you'll want to make it again on Christmas.*

YIELD: 8 SERVINGS

INGREDIENTS:
- 3 Tbsp. (45 ml) neutral-flavored oil
- 2 Tbsp. (19 g) all-purpose flour or garbanzo bean (chickpea) flour
- ¾ tsp. salt, plus more to taste
- ½ tsp. onion powder
- ¼ tsp. black pepper, plus more to taste
- 4 c. (448 g) fresh or frozen corn
- 1 ½ c. (356 ml) unsweetened, unflavored non-dairy milk, such as almond, cashew, or soy
- ½ c. (119 ml) canned full-fat coconut milk (shake can well before opening and stir well before measuring)
- 2 tsp. sugar
- Pinch of nutmeg
- Pinch of cayenne (optional)

FOR BEST GLUTEN FREE VERSION:
Use the garbanzo bean flour option instead of the regular all-purpose flour.

MAKE-AHEAD TIP:
This creamed corn can be made up to 2 days in advance and stored in an airtight container in the fridge. Reheat in a saucepan over medium-low heat until piping hot.

INSTRUCTIONS:
1. Heat the oil in a 3-quart or larger saucepan over medium heat. Add the flour, salt, onion powder, and pepper and cook 2–3 minutes, stirring frequently. Add the corn and stir well.

2. Add the milk, coconut milk, sugar, nutmeg, and cayenne, if using. Increase the heat to medium-high and stir until the mixture comes to a boil. Continue boiling an additional 1–2 minutes, or until slightly thickened.

3. Remove 1 c. (about one-fifth of the mixture) and transfer it to a blender or food processor. Pulse 8–10 times, or until corn is mostly smooth. Alternatively, the corn can be transferred to a small bowl and blended with an immersion blender. Return this mixture to the saucepan and stir well to combine with the rest of the corn.

4. Taste and season with salt and pepper as needed. Cover with a lid or plastic wrap until ready to serve. Serve hot.

# ROASTED ACORN SQUASH WITH GARLIC BUTTER SAUCE

*A hint of sweetness from the bright orange squash, a bit of richness and salt from the butter, and just the right amount of garlic to wake up those tastebuds. This side dish is super flavorful, all with a rustic presentation.*

YIELD: 6–8 SERVINGS

INGREDIENTS:
- 2 medium to large-sized acorn squashes, roughly equal in size
- 2 Tbsp. (30 ml) olive oil or avocado oil, plus more for roasting
- ½ tsp. salt, plus more for roasting
- ⅛ tsp. black pepper, plus more for roasting
- 2 Tbsp. (28 g) vegan butter or margarine
- 4 medium garlic cloves, minced
- ⅓ c. (43 g) finely chopped yellow onion
- ¾ c. (177 ml) low- sodium vegetable broth
- 1 Tbsp. (5 g) nutritional yeast flakes
- 1 pinch of red pepper flakes (optional)
- 1 small handful of fresh parsley, finely chopped

FOR BEST GLUTEN FREE VERSION:
This recipe is naturally gluten free, but check all ingredient labels to be sure.

MAKE-AHEAD TIP:
The acorn squash can be seeded and sliced into wedges up to 3 days in advance. Store wedges in an airtight container or resealable storage bag in the fridge until needed.

INSTRUCTIONS:
1. Preheat your oven to 375°F (approx. 190°C).
2. Halve both squashes lengthwise and scrape out the seeds with a spoon. Slice the squash into wedges, following the natural lines in the squash for guidance.
3. Place the wedges on a parchment-lined or nonstick baking sheet. Toss wedges with a light coating of oil, then lightly sprinkle both sides of each wedge with salt and pepper. Lay each wedge on its side for roasting.
4. Roast for 28–30 minutes, or until wedges are fork-tender and lightly browned, flipping each one over after 15 minutes.
5. Meanwhile, heat the oil and butter in a medium saucepan over medium-high heat. Once the butter is melted, add the garlic and onion and sauté until soft, about 2 minutes.
6. Pour in the broth and reduce the heat to medium-low. Add the nutritional yeast, salt, black pepper, and red pepper flakes, if using, and stir well. Simmer, stirring occasionally, until the sauce is slightly thickened, about 5 minutes.
7. Strain the sauce through a fine-mesh sieve or strainer. Discard the onion and garlic.
8. Arrange the acorn squash wedges on a platter or in a large serving bowl and drizzle garlic butter sauce evenly over the tops of the wedges. Garnish with finely chopped fresh parsley. Serve immediately.

NOTES:
- If your squash is too firm to cut, microwave the squashes for 4–5 minutes to help soften.
- This recipe can also be made with delicata squash, seeded and sliced.

# GREEN BEANS WITH ALMONDS AND CARAMELIZED SHALLOTS

*This is truly my favorite green bean recipe. The caramelized shallots, crunchy toasted almonds, and juicy green beans are a trio made in heaven. After trying this dish, you may never want to prepare green beans any other way.*

YIELD: ABOUT 6 SERVINGS

INGREDIENTS:
- ¼ c. (28 g) sliced almonds
- 1 Tbsp. (15 ml) olive oil or avocado oil
- 2 medium shallots, thinly sliced
- 1 lb. (454 g) fresh green beans, trimmed (the thin French type, if possible)
- 1 tsp. rice vinegar or white distilled vinegar
- ¼ tsp. salt, plus more to taste
- ⅛ tsp. black pepper, plus more to taste

FOR BEST GLUTEN FREE VERSION:
This recipe is naturally gluten free, but check all ingredient labels to be sure.

MAKE-AHEAD TIP:
The almonds can be toasted and cooled, the shallots can be sliced, and the green beans can be blanched and cooled 1 day ahead. Store all three in separate airtight containers or resealable storage bags. Store the almonds at room temperature and the shallots and green beans in the fridge until needed.

INSTRUCTIONS:
1. In a large skillet, toast the almonds over medium heat until fragrant and lightly browned, about 5 minutes. Transfer immediately to a paper towel or plate.

2. Wipe that skillet with a clean towel to remove any almond pieces or dust (keep in mind the pan will be hot), then return to medium heat. Add the oil and heat for about 15 seconds.

3. Add the shallot slices and turn the heat down to medium-low. Cover the skillet with a lid and cook the shallots, stirring frequently, until medium brown and caramelized. This can take anywhere from 5–15 minutes, depending on the thickness of the slices.

4. Meanwhile, bring a large pot or saucepan filled with water to a boil. Once boiling, add the green beans all at once and cook for about 3 minutes to blanch, or until they're bright green and tender, yet slightly crisp.

5. Drain the green beans well and transfer them to the skillet containing the shallots. Add the vinegar, salt, and pepper and toss to combine and coat the green beans. Give the green beans a taste and add more salt and pepper, if desired.

6. Transfer to a large bowl or platter and sprinkle the toasted almonds over the top. Serve immediately.

# THYME-ROASTED CARROTS

*Easy-to-make and filled with fresh, seasonal flavors, these thyme roasted carrots prove a recipe doesn't need to be complicated to be impressive.*

YIELD: 8 SERVINGS

INGREDIENTS:

- 2 lb. (908 g) medium to large-sized carrots
- 2 Tbsp. (30 ml) olive oil or avocado oil
- 1 Tbsp. (15 ml) maple syrup
- 2 tsp. finely chopped fresh thyme
- ½ tsp. salt, plus more to taste
- ¼ tsp black pepper, plus more to taste

FOR BEST GLUTEN FREE VERSION:
This recipe is naturally gluten free, but check all ingredient labels to be sure.

MAKE-AHEAD TIP:
The carrots can be sliced and stored in an airtight container or resealable storage bag up to 2 days in advance. Simply store in the refrigerator until needed, then allow to sit at room temperature for about 20 minutes before using.

INSTRUCTIONS:

1. Preheat your oven to 400°F (approx. 204°C).
2. Slice the carrots into 1 ½-inch (about 4-cm) pieces. For any wider carrots, slice in half lengthwise before slicing into pieces. Note: Peeling is optional. I usually leave the peel on for this recipe.
3. Place the carrots in a mixing bowl and add all the remaining ingredients. Toss to evenly coat each slice.
4. Transfer the carrots to a parchment-lined or nonstick baking sheet.
5. Roast just until fork-tender yet still slightly crisp, 15–20 minutes depending on the thickness of the carrots.
6. Add extra salt and pepper to taste. Serve hot.

NOTE:
Fresh thyme is best in this recipe, so do not substitute dried thyme.

# APPLE WALNUT SALAD WITH CINNAMON CIDER DRESSING

*With so many rich, savory and warm dishes included in the Thanksgiving spread, I love serving a fresh, cool salad on this holiday. Not only to offer a bit of variety on our plates, but also to cleanse our palates between bites of the traditional goodness we're enjoying.*

YIELD: 4–6 SERVINGS

INGREDIENTS:

**Maple Walnuts:**
- ½ c. (47 g) walnut halves, roughly chopped
- 2 ½ Tbsp. (40 ml) maple syrup
- A couple pinches of salt

**Cinnamon Cider Dressing:**
- ⅓ c. (79 ml) apple cider vinegar
- ⅓ c. (79 ml) maple syrup
- 2 Tbsp. (30 ml) neutral-flavored oil (optional)
- 1 tsp. Dijon mustard
- ½ tsp. cinnamon
- Pinch of salt
- Pinch of fresh ground black pepper (optional)

**Salad:**
- 3 c. (78g) packed curly kale, chopped into small ½-inch (about 1.5-cm) pieces
- 4 c. (152 g) packed chopped romaine lettuce
- 1 sweet apple (such as Fuji or Gala), cored and chopped (leave skin on for color)
- ⅓ c. (43 g) dried cranberries, roughly chopped

INSTRUCTIONS:

1. To make the Maple Walnuts, place a skillet on the stove over medium-high heat. Once hot, add the walnuts to the pan to toast. While nuts are toasting, place a sheet of parchment paper and a metal spoon nearby.

2. Once the nuts are fragrant and a slightly darker color, add the maple syrup to the pan. Quickly grab the metal spoon and stir the nuts and syrup together. Continue stirring until most of the syrup has stuck to the nuts, 10–15 seconds. Immediately remove the pan from the heat and carefully pour the nuts onto the parchment paper in a single layer.

3. While the nuts are still warm, sprinkle evenly with a pinch or two of salt. Once cool, break them apart so they're no longer stuck together. Set aside for now.

4. To make the Cinnamon Cider Dressing, combine all the ingredients in a mason jar, close the lid tightly, and shake to combine. Alternatively, you can whisk the ingredients together in a bowl.

5. To assemble the salad, combine the kale and half of the dressing in a mixing bowl and firmly massage the dressing into the kale with your fingertips for at least 30 seconds to help tenderize the kale. Then add the romaine and gently toss until all the lettuce is evenly coated. Transfer the dressed greens to your serving bowl or platter of choice and drizzle with the desired amount of the remaining dressing. Note: You may not need all of it.

Recipe continues

**FOR BEST GLUTEN FREE VERSION:**
This recipe is naturally gluten free, but check all ingredient labels to be sure.

**MAKE-AHEAD TIP:**
The Maple Walnuts can be made up to 2 days in advance, completely cooled, and stored in an airtight container at room temperature until needed. The Cinnamon Cider Dressing can be made up to 4 days in advance and stored in the fridge until needed. The kale can be chopped and massaged with dressing one day ahead. The romaine can be chopped and placed in a mixing bowl covered in plastic wrap the morning of the day the salad will be served. Keep all greens in the fridge until needed.

6.  Top the dressed greens with, in this order, the apple, dried cranberries, and lastly the walnuts. Leaving these ingredients on top rather than tossing them in creates a pretty presentation and shows your guests what flavors they can expect to enjoy in this salad.

**NOTES:**
- Feel free to use other types of lettuce, if you like. Keep in mind that kale is the only type that needs to be "massaged" with dressing, as mentioned in step 5.
- Other types of nuts can be used in place of the walnuts. Pecans are a great option.
- For sweeter salad dressing, skip the oil option. For a richer, slightly less-sweet dressing, however, be sure to include it.
- Consider serving your salad in a chilled bowl to help keep the salad cool among all the piping hot dishes in your Thanksgiving spread.

# CRAVE-WORTHY SOUTHERN GREENS

*Get ready for some immense flavor with these tender collard greens! This recipe manages to incorporate a little heat, a bit of sweet, and just the right amount of acid coming from the relish and a splash of vinegar.*

YIELD: 4 SERVINGS

INGREDIENTS:
- 2 bunches (about 415 g) fresh collard greens
- 2 Tbsp. (30 ml) olive oil or avocado oil
- 1 medium white or yellow onion, chopped
- ¾ tsp. salt, divided
- 1 c. (237 ml) water, plus more as needed
- 2 Tbsp. (30 ml) rice vinegar or white distilled vinegar
- 1 Tbsp. (14 g) granulated sugar
- ½ tsp. paprika
- ½ tsp. crushed red pepper (or ¼ tsp for mild heat)
- ½ tsp. garlic powder
- 3 Tbsp. (45 g) dill pickle relish or chow-chow
- ¼ tsp. black pepper

FOR BEST GLUTEN FREE VERSION:
This recipe is naturally gluten free, but check all ingredient labels to be sure.

MAKE-AHEAD TIP:
This entire dish can be made, cooled, and stored in an airtight container in the fridge up to 2 days in advance. Simply warm in a saucepan on the stove over medium heat before serving.

INSTRUCTIONS:
1. Remove and discard tough stems from the greens. Then roll the leaves up tightly and slice into ½–1-inch (1.5–3-cm) ribbons.
2. In a large pot, heat the oil over medium heat for about 30 seconds. Add the chopped onion and ¼ tsp. salt and cook, stirring occasionally, until soft and light brown, 5–7 minutes.
3. Reduce the heat to medium-low and add the collard greens, water, vinegar, sugar, paprika, crushed red pepper, and garlic powder. Cook, stirring occasionally, until greens are very tender, 20–25 minutes. If the greens seem dry, add water ¼ c. (59 ml) at a time as needed.
4. Stir in the relish or chow-chow, remaining ½ tsp. salt, and the black pepper. Serve warm or hot.

# CREAMY MAC AND CHEESE

*This macaroni with velvety cheese sauce is a fun way to sneak a flavor-punch of cheese into what is traditionally a cheese-free feast. I'm willing to bet that even the biggest fans of mac and cheese will have trouble detecting that this version is dairy-free.*

YIELD: 12 SERVINGS

INGREDIENTS:
- ½ c. (113 g) vegan butter or margarine, plus more for greasing
- ¼ c. + 2 Tbsp. (53 g) all-purpose flour, or ¼ c. + 2 Tbsp. (48 g) tapioca starch
- 3 ½ c. (830 ml) unsweetened, unflavored non-dairy milk, such as almond, cashew, or soy
- ¾ c. (177 ml) low-sodium vegetable broth
- ¼ c. (20 g) nutritional yeast flakes
- 1 vegetable bouillon cube (or 1 tsp. bouillon substitute)
- ½ tsp. paprika
- ¼ tsp. salt, plus more to taste
- ⅛ tsp. black pepper, plus more to taste
- 2 c. (240 g) shredded vegan cheddar cheese, plus more to taste
- 16 oz. (454 g) elbow macaroni noodles

FOR BEST GLUTEN FREE VERSION:
Use the tapioca starch option instead of the regular all-purpose flour, and use gluten free elbow macaroni noodles.

MAKE-AHEAD TIP:
This dish is best served the day it's made; however, you can make it up to 1 hour prior to serving time. Keep it in the saucepan and cover with a lid or plastic wrap, stirring occasionally. Reheat a few minutes over medium heat before serving, if needed.

INSTRUCTIONS:
1. Melt the butter in a 3-quart or larger saucepan over medium-high heat. Add the flour or starch and whisk until all flour is incorporated.
2. Add the non-dairy milk and broth and whisk until it becomes bubbly. Continue whisking as it boils until the mixture starts to thicken, about 5 minutes. Keep in mind, it will thicken quite a bit more after all the remaining ingredients are added.
3. Remove the pan from the heat and add the nutritional yeast flakes, vegetable bouillon, paprika, salt, and pepper and stir well. Once combined, whisk in the vegan cheese. Note: You may need to place the pan back over low heat for the cheese to completely melt. It may take several minutes of whisking to become smooth.
4. Carefully taste and add more cheese for a cheesier flavor, and add salt and pepper to taste. Cover and set sauce aside for now.
5. Cook the elbow pasta in boiling water according to the package directions. Drain well and add the pasta to the pot containing the sauce. Stir to coat all the macaroni noodles. Add salt to taste. Serve hot.

NOTE:
If sensitive to salt, use low-sodium vegetable bouillon cubes. You can always add more salt to taste afterward.

# PERFECT CRANBERRY SAUCE

*Nothing brightens a Thanksgiving plate like a heaping spoonful of glorious cranberry sauce! The addition of orange zest and fruit juice takes this cranberry sauce recipe to the next level. In fact, my son James enjoys eating a bowl of this cranberry sauce all on its own!*

**YIELD: 6–8 SERVINGS**

**INGREDIENTS:**

- 12 oz. (340 g) fresh or frozen whole cranberries
- 1 c. (230 g) granulated sugar
- 2 Tbsp. (30 ml) orange juice or apple cider
- 1 tsp. orange zest
- 1 pinch of cinnamon (optional)
- 1 pinch of ground cloves (optional)

**FOR BEST GLUTEN FREE VERSION:**
This recipe is naturally gluten free, but check all ingredient labels to be sure.

**MAKE-AHEAD TIP:**
This cranberry sauce can be made up to 3 days in advance. Store in the refrigerator in an airtight container or in a bowl covered in plastic wrap.

**INSTRUCTIONS:**

1. Sort through the cranberries and pull out any that are smashed or rotten. If using fresh cranberries, give them a thorough rinse as well.

2. Measure out ½ c. (52 g) of the cranberries and set them aside for now.

3. Place the remaining cranberries in a medium saucepan along with the sugar, juice, and orange zest. Cook over medium-low heat, stirring occasionally, until the sugar dissolves, 10–12 minutes.

4. Increase the heat to medium and cook until the cranberries burst, another 10–12 minutes.

5. Reduce the heat to medium-low and add the reserved cranberries. Cook 3–4 minutes, or until the reserved cranberries appear slightly soft. Stir in a pinch or two of cinnamon and/or ground cloves, if desired.

6. Immediately transfer to a bowl and allow the cranberry sauce to cool to room temperature, then transfer to the refrigerator to chill completely, about 4 hours or overnight. Remove from the refrigerator 10–15 minutes before serving.

**NOTE:**
If you like, water can be used in place of the orange juice or apple cider.

# CLASSIC BROWN GRAVY

*Since many like to drizzle their entire Thanksgiving plate with gravy, a solid gravy recipe is a must! This is the version that our family enjoys most; it offers hints of onion and garlic with just a wink of thyme, sage, and black pepper, too.*

YIELD: ABOUT 8 SERVINGS

INGREDIENTS:
- 2 ½ c. (593 ml) low-sodium vegetable broth, divided
- 3 Tbsp. (24 g) cornstarch
- 1 Tbsp. (15 ml) soy sauce or substitute
- ¾ tsp. onion powder
- ½ tsp. garlic powder
- ¼ tsp. dried thyme
- ¼ tsp. dried sage
- ¼ tsp. black pepper, plus more to taste
- ¼ c. (57 g) vegan butter or margarine
- Pinch of salt, if needed

FOR BEST GLUTEN FREE VERSION:
Use gluten free soy sauce or gluten free soy sauce alternative.

MAKE-AHEAD TIP:
This gravy is best served immediately after it is made. However, it can be made up to 1 hour before serving time and kept in a saucepan covered with a lid over very low heat. Whisk occasionally until ready to serve.

INSTRUCTIONS:
1. Combine ½ c. (119 ml) of the vegetable broth and the cornstarch in a small bowl and whisk with a fork until smooth. Add the soy sauce, onion powder, garlic powder, thyme, sage, and black pepper and whisk again until all the lumps are gone.
2. Melt the butter in a saucepan over medium-high heat.
3. Add the cornstarch mixture and whisk until bubbly and very hot. It will likely be clumpy.
4. Very slowly add the remaining 2 c. (474 ml) of broth, whisking as you pour. Bring this mixture to a boil and then reduce the heat to a simmer. Continue simmering until desired thickness is reached. It may only take 1–2 minutes, but could take longer. Add salt and pepper to taste. Serve hot.

# BREAD AND
# BUTTER

# SOFT DINNER ROLLS

*My mouth waters at even the thought of these soft and pillowy dinner rolls! They are a crowd favorite in the Dunham household, and truly worth every minute required to make them.*

YIELD: 20 ROLLS

INGREDIENTS:
- ⅓ c. + 2 ½ Tbsp. (110 g) vegan butter or margarine, divided
- 2 c. (474 ml) unsweetened, unflavored non-dairy milk, such as almond, cashew, or soy
- ½ c. (119 ml) water
- ⅓ c. + 1 Tbsp. (86 g) granulated sugar
- 2 ¼ tsp. (one 7-g packet) dry active yeast
- 2 tsp. salt
- 5 ½–6 c. (770–840 g) all-purpose flour, plus more as needed
- Neutral-flavored oil for greasing

MAKE-AHEAD TIP:
The rolls can be made up to 2 days in advance. Allow them to cool completely and then store in resealable plastic bags or an airtight container at room temperature until needed.

INSTRUCTIONS:
1. Heat ⅓ c. + 1 Tbsp. (85 g) of the vegan butter in a small saucepan over low heat until melted. Add the milk and water and continue heating until hot (like bathwater) but not scalding, 105–110°F (approx. 40–43°C).

2. Pour this mixture into the bowl of your stand mixer. Add the sugar and stir to combine. If you have a thermometer on hand, check the temperature again to ensure the mixture is between 100 and 110°F (approx. 37–43°C). The liquid should be hot, but not hot enough to sting. (Too hot and it will kill the yeast, too cool and it will not activate it.)

3. Add the yeast to the bowl and stir to combine. Let sit for 5–10 minutes, or until bubbly white "clouds" form across the surface and it has a strong yeasty aroma, then stir in the salt.

4. Using the dough hook attachment on low speed, add the flour 1 c. (140 g) at a time until the dough has come together and is tacky and stretchy but not overly sticky (a little sticky is okay!). You may feel you have enough flour after just 5 ½ c. (770 g). It's best not to add too much flour.

5. Increase the speed to medium and knead the dough for 5–6 minutes, until it is smooth, stretchy, and a little sticky.

6. Grease a large bowl with oil. Transfer the dough to the bowl and cover with a clean kitchen towel. Let sit at room temperature far away from sunlight or a hot stove or oven until the dough has doubled in size, 40–60 minutes. In the meantime, grease a 9-x-13-inch (23-x-33-cm) baking dish with oil.

7. Remove the towel and punch the dough right down the center. Then sprinkle a clean, flat surface with flour and turn the dough out onto that surface. The dough may still be a little sticky, but it should be smooth and soft for the most part. Note: Keep flour nearby and lightly flour your hands, work surface, and the dough as needed throughout the next step.

Recipe continues

8. Using a dough scraper or large knife, quarter the dough, then cut each quarter into five relatively equal-sized pieces (they don't need to be exact). Tuck the sides of each piece of dough under itself to create round dough balls. Place them on your greased dish to create five rows of four balls. Cover the dough balls with plastic wrap and allow them to rise once again very far away from sunlight or a hot stove or oven until almost doubled in size, 25–35 minutes. Meanwhile, preheat your oven to 375°F (approx. 190°F).

9. Melt the last 1 ½ Tbsp. (21 g) butter and gently brush it over the surface of the dough balls.

10. Bake for 25–35 minutes, or until each and every roll has turned a medium brown color. It's best to rotate your pan halfway through baking.

11. Remove from the oven and allow to cool at least 10 minutes before serving. Rolls can be served hot or room temperature.

NOTE:
The dough can also be made by hand if you don't have access to a stand mixer. Simply add the flour to the bowl one cup at a time, stirring to incorporate. Then knead by hand on a flat, floured surface for about 6 minutes rather than using the mixer.

# LOADED SKILLET CORNBREAD

*Baking this recipe in cast iron results in cornbread with golden crispy-chewy edges that perfectly complement the cheesiness and smokiness in the bread itself. (But honestly, doesn't everything taste better when made in a cast iron skillet?)*

YIELD: 8–10 SERVINGS

INGREDIENTS:
- 6 strips vegan bacon
- 1 ½ c. (356 ml) unsweetened, unflavored, non-dairy milk such as cashew, almond, or soy
- 1 ½ Tbsp. (23 ml) rice vinegar or white distilled vinegar
- 2 c. (314 g) cornmeal
- ½ c. (70 g) all-purpose flour
- 2 tsp. granulated sugar
- 1 tsp. salt
- 1 tsp. baking powder
- 1 tsp. baking soda
- ¾ tsp. onion powder
- ¾ tsp. garlic powder
- ½ tsp. paprika
- ¼ tsp. cayenne
- ½ c. (119 ml) neutral-flavored oil, divided
- ¾ c. (90 g) vegan shredded cheddar cheese
- ⅔ c. (75 g) corn, fresh or frozen and thawed
- 1 (4 oz. / 113 g) can diced green chiles, excess liquid drained

FOR BEST GLUTEN FREE VERSION:
Use your favorite gluten free all-purpose flour in place of the regular all-purpose flour, and add ½ tsp. xanthan gum (if your flour mix doesn't already contain it). Check the labels for all remaining ingredients to ensure they're gluten free, particularly the bacon.

INSTRUCTIONS:
1. Preheat your oven to 450°F (approx. 232°C) and place a well-seasoned 10-inch (25-cm) cast iron skillet on the top rack.
2. Cook the vegan bacon strips in a separate skillet over medium-high heat on the stove until lightly browned on both sides. Once cool enough to handle, chop or tear bacon into roughly ¼–½-inch (0.5–1.5-cm) pieces. Set aside for now.
3. In a small bowl, combine the milk and vinegar and give the mixture a good stir. (It will start to curdle, and that's what you want!) Set this aside as well.
4. In a large bowl, stir together the cornmeal, flour, sugar, salt, baking powder, baking soda, onion powder, garlic powder, paprika, and cayenne.
5. Add ¼ c. (59 ml) oil and the milk mixture to the bowl and stir well until just combined.
6. Fold in the shredded cheese, corn, chiles, and chopped bacon. Allow the batter to rest for 5 minutes.
7. Add the remaining ¼ c. (59 ml) of oil to the hot cast iron skillet and let heat for 20–30 seconds, then pour in the batter and spread into an even layer.
8. Bake for 25 minutes, or until the edges are golden brown and a toothpick inserted in the center comes out batter-free. Let the cornbread rest for 5 minutes before serving. This cornbread is best served fresh and warm.

NOTE:
This cornbread is best made in a cast iron skillet. However, it can also be made in a 2-quart dish such as a 7-x-11-inch (18-x-28-cm) baking dish. For this option, do not heat the dish ahead of time or add the ¼ c. of oil to the dish before baking. Instead, liberally grease your room-temperature baking dish before adding the batter.

MAKE-AHEAD TIP:
All dry ingredients, including the cornmeal, flour, sugar, baking powder, baking soda, and spices, can be measured out, mixed together, and stored in an airtight container up to 3 days in advance. Store at room temperature until needed.

# SWEET CORNBREAD

*This cornbread recipe has been a favorite of mine for years and it has graced our holiday spreads many times, typically in muffin form (see Notes). In fact, my son Jack often eats two or three muffins at a time! The added bonus is this sweet cornbread can be made in about 30 minutes.*

YIELD: 8–12 SERVINGS

INGREDIENTS:

- 1 ¼ c. (296 ml) unsweetened, unflavored, non-dairy milk such as cashew, almond, or soy
- 1 Tbsp. (15 ml) apple cider vinegar, rice vinegar, or white distilled vinegar
- 1 ¼ c. (196 g) cornmeal
- ¾ c. (105 g) all-purpose flour
- 1 Tbsp. (12 g) baking powder
- 1 tsp. salt
- ½ c. (119 ml) maple syrup
- ¼ c. (59 ml) neutral-flavored oil, plus more for greasing

FOR BEST GLUTEN FREE VERSION:

Use your favorite gluten free all-purpose flour in place of the regular all-purpose flour, and add ½ tsp. xanthan gum (if your flour mix doesn't already contain it) to the dry ingredients in step 3. Check the labels for all remaining ingredients to ensure they're gluten free.

MAKE-AHEAD TIP:

If baking in a 2-quart dish, the cornbread can be made 1 day in advance, cooled completely, and then stored away from heat and loosely covered in plastic wrap until needed. If making muffins instead, they are best baked the morning of the day they will be served.

INSTRUCTIONS:

1. Preheat your oven to 350°F (approx. 177°C). Grease a 7-x-11-inch (18-x-28-cm) baking dish with oil. Set aside.

2. Combine the milk and vinegar in a small bowl and give the mixture a good stir. (It will start to curdle, and that's what you want!) Set this aside as well.

3. In a mixing bowl, whisk together the cornmeal, flour, baking powder, and salt.

4. Add the maple syrup, oil, and milk mixture to the bowl and whisk until well combined, breaking up any clumps along the way.

5. Pour the batter into the prepared baking dish. Bake for 28–30 minutes, or until the center feels very firm to the touch and a toothpick inserted in the center comes out batter-free.

NOTE:

To make muffins instead, line a muffin tin or two with 13 liners (you may only need 12) and fill each one two-thirds full with batter. Use an ice cream scoop to help with the process. Bake at 350°F (approx. 177°C) for 20–22 minutes, or until a toothpick inserted in the center of one or two muffins comes out batter-free.

# BUTTERMILK BISCUITS

*Bake these buttermilk biscuits for your Thanksgiving only if you wish to have your guests singing your praises! This recipe results in golden-brown biscuits with layers of soft goodness, all with that distinctly wonderful biscuit aroma and flavor.*

YIELD: 10–12 BISCUITS

INGREDIENTS:

- 1 c. (237 ml) unsweetened, unflavored, non-dairy milk such as cashew, almond, or soy, plus more for brushing
- 1 Tbsp. (15 ml) rice vinegar or distilled white vinegar
- 2 ⅓ c. (327 g) all-purpose flour
- 2 Tbsp. (24 g) baking powder
- 1 tsp. salt
- ½ c. (113 g) cold vegan butter or margarine, cut into ½-inch (1.5-cm) cubes, plus 1 Tbsp. (14 g) melted, for topping
- 2 tsp. maple syrup

INSTRUCTIONS:

1. Preheat your oven to 425°F (approx. 218°C).

2. Combine the milk and vinegar in a small bowl. Give it a good stir. (It will start to curdle, and that's what you want!) Set this aside.

3. In a mixing bowl, combine the flour, baking powder, and salt, and stir well to mix. (Alternatively, you can use a food processor for steps 3 and 4.)

4. Add the cold butter cubes and cut in with a pastry cutter or a large fork, or pulse in the food processor. If using a food processor, transfer the contents to a large bowl after the butter is incorporated.

5. Make a well in the center of the flour and pour the milk mixture right in the middle. Add the maple syrup. Fold the ingredients together with a rubber spatula or large spoon until the dough starts to come together. Do not overwork the dough. It should look shaggy with some wet spots.

6. Pour the dough out onto a floured, flat surface and gently bring it together with well-floured hands. The dough will be sticky, so keep extra flour nearby to re-flour your hands, rolling pin, and work surface throughout the next steps.

7. Using a floured rolling pin, roll the dough into a ¾-inch-thick (about 2-cm) rectangle. Fold one short side into the center, then fold the opposite short side over the top of that, like folding a letter. Use a bench scraper or a large sharp knife if needed to assist with folding. If the dough is sticking to the surface, sprinkle flour as needed.

8. Turn the dough so it is horizontal and roll it out again into a ¾-inch-thick (about 2-cm) rectangle. Once again, fold one of the short sides into the center, then fold the opposite side over the top.

9. Repeat Step 8 two more times, handling the dough gently and minimally throughout the process. Then flatten the dough one last time into a ¾-inch-thick (about 2-cm) rectangle.

Recipe continues

**FOR BEST GLUTEN FREE VERSION:**
See next recipe for gluten free drop
biscuits.

**MAKE-AHEAD TIP:**
Prepare the dough up until Step 9,
then wrap it tightly with plastic wrap
and store in the refrigerator for up to
2 days. The day you plan to enjoy the
biscuits, continue with steps 10–13.

10. Using a 2 ½–3-inch (about 7–7.5-cm) round cutter, cut as many
    circles as you can into the dough, pressing straight down into the
    dough without twisting.

11. Re-roll the scraps and continue cutting circles until the doug
    is used up. You should have roughly 10–12 biscuits in the end.

12. Arrange the biscuits on a parchment-lined baking sheet close
    enough that their edges touch one another (this will help
    maintain their shape while baking.) Alternatively, you can place
    them in a greased cast iron skillet. Lightly brush the surface of
    the biscuits with non-dairy milk.

13. Bake for 14–18 minutes, or until the tops are light golden brown.
    Remove from the oven and brush the tops with melted butter.
    These biscuits are best when served the day they are baked.

# GLUTEN FREE DROP BISCUITS

*No need to skip the bread if you're having a gluten free Thanksgiving! These drop biscuits are simple to make and are delightfully delicious. We're big fans of this recipe in our home (even though we don't require gluten free foods), and love topping our biscuits with Maple Butter (page 90).*

YIELD: 10–12 BISCUITS

INGREDIENTS:

- 1 c. + ½ Tbsp. (245 ml) unsweetened, unflavored non-dairy milk, such as almond, cashew, or soy, divided
- 1 Tbsp. (15 ml) white distilled vinegar
- 1 ¾ c. (280 g) gluten free all-purpose flour
- ¾ tsp. xanthan gum (omit if your flour mix contains it)
- ¼ c. (32 g) cornstarch
- 1 Tbsp. (12 g) baking powder
- 1 Tbsp. (14 g) granulated sugar
- ¼ tsp. plus 1 pinch salt, divided
- ½ c. (113 g) cold vegan butter or margarine, cut into ¼-inch (about 0.5-cm) cubes
- ½ Tbsp. neutral-flavored oil

MAKE-AHEAD TIP:

These biscuits are best served the day they are made. However, they can be baked the morning of the day you plan to serve them. Once completely cooled, keep them in a bowl tented with foil (not plastic wrap) until ready to serve

INSTRUCTIONS:

1. Preheat your oven to 425°F (approx. 218°C).
2. In a small bowl, combine 1 c. (237 ml) of the milk and the vinegar and stir well to mix. (It will curdle, and that's what you want!) Set aside.
3. In a large mixing bowl, whisk together the flour, xanthan gum (if using), cornstarch, baking powder, sugar, and ¼ tsp. salt.
4. Cut in the cold butter cubes with a pastry cutter or your fingertips until the butter pieces are pea- to bean-sized.
5. Create a well in the center of the dry ingredients and add the milk mixture. Gently stir until just combined.
6. Using an ice cream scoop or ¼-c. measure, drop 10–12 dough mounds about 2 inches (5 cm) apart from one another on a parchment-lined or nonstick baking sheet. Press the tops slightly to flatten them a bit.
7. In a small bowl or ramekin, combine the remaining ½ Tbsp. milk, the oil, and a pinch of salt. Lightly brush the top of each mound of dough with this mixture.
8. Bake for 15–16 minutes, rotating halfway through, until the biscuits are lightly golden brown all over. Allow them to set for about 5 minutes before serving.

NOTES:

- For this recipe, I recommend using a gluten free all-purpose flour that lists white rice flour as the first ingredient.
- If wheat gluten is not an issue for you and your group, you can certainly make these drop biscuits with 1 ¾ c. (245 g) regular all-purpose flour, if you like! In this case, omit the xanthan gum, as you will no longer need it.

# MAPLE BUTTER

*One way to make your guests feel extra special is to offer a variety of butters on Thanksgiving. This maple butter goes wonderfully on rolls, biscuits, and cornbread, offering a sweet and rich maple flavor. I prefer serving my maple butter in several small ramekins placed across the dining room table to make it easily accessible for everyone.*

YIELD: ABOUT 8 SERVINGS

INGREDIENTS:
- ½ c. (113 g) vegan butter or margarine, softened
- ⅓ c. (65 g) powdered sugar (confectioners' sugar), sifted, plus more to taste
- ¼ tsp. maple extract
- ¼ tsp. cinnamon

MAKE-AHEAD TIP:
This butter can be made and stored in the fridge for 3–4 weeks, but I personally feel it is best if enjoyed within a week.

INSTRUCTIONS:
1. Combine all the ingredients in a mixing bowl. Using a handheld or stand mixer, mix on medium-low speed until combined and creamy. Scrape the sides and bottom of the bowl as needed. Give the butter a try and add more powdered sugar one small spoonful at a time until desired sweetness level is reached.

2. Place the bowl in the refrigerator to chill for 20 minutes.

3. Transfer the chilled butter to the center of a sheet of plastic wrap, parchment, or wax paper. Use the plastic or paper to roll the butter into a log, twisting the ends and tucking them under. Alternatively, the butter can be placed in one large or four small ramekins, if you'd like to serve it that way. Cover the ramekins in plastic wrap for the time being.

4. Chill for an additional hour, or until butter is needed. Let sit at room temperature for at least 15 minutes before serving.

# TRUFFLE BUTTER

*If you're looking to be placed in the "rock star" category of hosting, offer your guests truffle butter to accompany their creamy mashed potatoes and fresh bread. The umami factor of the meal will be elevated dramatically, and your guests are likely to never forget it. The added bonus is that truffle butter is unbelievably easy to make.*

YIELD: ABOUT 8 SERVINGS

INGREDIENTS:
- ½ c. (113 g) vegan butter or margarine, softened
- 1 small (roughly ¼-oz. / 7–9-g) white or black truffle

MAKE-AHEAD TIP:
This butter can be made and stored in the fridge for 3–4 weeks, but I personally feel it is best if enjoyed within a week.

INSTRUCTIONS:
1. Place the butter in a mixing bowl.
2. Using a microplane, zester, or the smallest holes on your grater, grate the truffle directly over the butter.
3. Mash together with a fork until well combined.
4. Place the bowl in the refrigerator to chill for 20 minutes.
5. Transfer the chilled butter to the center of a sheet of plastic wrap, parchment, or wax paper. Use the plastic or paper to roll the butter into a log, twisting the ends and tucking them under. Alternatively, the butter can be placed in one large or four small ramekins, if you'd like to serve it that way. Cover the ramekins in plastic wrap for the time being.
6. Chill for an additional hour, or until butter is needed. Let sit at room temperature for at least 15 minutes before serving.

# PIES AND TOPPINGS

# SINGLE PIE CRUST

*At the base of every great pie is a great crust. I've used this crust recipe time and time again, and it always results in a stable crust with crunchy yet tender edges, lightly salted flavor, and just a whisper of sweetness. I hope you love it as much as we do!*

YIELD: 1 PIE CRUST

INGREDIENTS:
- 1 ⅓ c. (187 g) all-purpose flour, plus more as needed
- 1 Tbsp. (14 g) granulated sugar
- ½ tsp. salt
- ½ c. (77 g) vegetable shortening
- ¼ c. (59 ml) ice water, plus more as needed

FOR BEST GLUTEN FREE VERSION:
Use the recipe for Gluten Free Single Pie Crust (page 96) instead.

MAKE-AHEAD TIP:
The dough disc can be made in advance and stored in the fridge for up to 4 days, or in the freezer wrapped in two layers of plastic wrap for up to 1 month.

INSTRUCTIONS:
1. In the bowl of a food processor, combine the flour, sugar, and salt and pulse several times to combine.
2. Add the shortening one spoonful at a time, spreading the shortening pieces out rather than adding one big mound.
3. Pulse a few times until the pieces of shortening are small (pea- to bean-sized) and covered in flour.
4. Add the ice water and pulse a couple more times, just until the dough starts to come together.
5. Transfer this mixture to a flat, lightly floured surface and begin gathering the pieces together with your hands. Form a disc shape, all while trying to handle the dough as little as possible. Note: If the dough feels overly sticky, knead in a few extra pinches of flour. If the dough feels overly dry, knead in extra ice water a few drops at a time, all while aiming to handle the dough as little as possible.
6. Smooth over the surface of the disc and wrap it in plastic wrap. Use your hands to then smooth over any cracks in the dough.
7. Place the disc in the fridge to chill for at least 40 minutes. When ready to use it, remove from the fridge and let sit at room temperature until the dough becomes pliable yet is still cool. If it becomes too warm, return it to the fridge for a couple of minutes.
8. Place the disc on a lightly floured surface and roll into a circle about ⅛ inch (0.25 cm) thick. Lightly sprinkle flour on your dough and rolling pin as needed to prevent sticking. Carefully wrap the dough circle around your rolling pin and unroll it across the top of a 9-inch (23-cm) pie plate. Press the sides and bottom to secure the dough to the pie plate. Fold the top edges under themselves and press down to firmly secure to the rim of the pie plate. Crimp the edges as desired.

TO PAR-BAKE THE CRUST:
Place the pie plate on a baking sheet and pierce the sides and bottom of the crust several times with a fork. Bake in a 400°F (approx. 204°C) oven for 10 minutes, rotating the plate halfway through baking.

TO BLIND-BAKE THE CRUST:
Place the pie plate on a baking sheet and pierce the sides and bottom of the crust several times with a fork. Bake in a 400°F (approx. 204°C) oven for 18–20 minutes, or until edges are lightly browned and the sides and bottom appear to be fully cooked. Rotate the plate halfway through baking.

# DOUBLE PIE CRUST

*Whether you're making a pie that requires a top crust such as my Country Apple Pie (page 102), or a grand dessert that needs a large bottom crust, such as my Caramel Apple Crumble Slab Pie (page 111), this double pie crust recipe is exactly what you need to get the job done in the most delicious way!*

YIELD: 2 PIE CRUSTS

INGREDIENTS:
- 2 ⅔ c. (373 g) all-purpose flour, plus more as needed
- 2 Tbsp. (28 g) granulated sugar
- 1 tsp. salt
- 1 c. (153 g) vegetable shortening
- ½ c. (119 ml) ice water, plus more as needed

FOR BEST GLUTEN FREE VERSION:
Use the recipe for Gluten Free Double Pie Crust (page 97) instead.

MAKE-AHEAD TIP:
The dough disc can be made in advance and stored in the fridge for up to 4 days, or in the freezer wrapped in 2 layers of plastic wrap for up to 1 month.

INSTRUCTIONS:
1. In the bowl of a food processor, combine the flour, sugar, and salt and pulse several times to combine.
2. Add the shortening one spoonful at a time, spreading the shortening pieces out rather than adding one big mound.
3. Pulse a few times until the pieces of shortening are small (pea- to bean-sized) and covered in flour.
4. Add the ice water and pulse a couple more times, just until the dough starts to come together.
5. Transfer this mixture to a flat, lightly floured surface and begin gathering the pieces together with your hands. Form a large disc shape, all while trying to handle the dough as little as possible. Note: If the dough feels overly sticky, knead in a few extra pinches of flour. If the dough feels overly dry, gently knead in extra ice water a few drops at a time, all while aiming to handle the dough as little as possible.
6. Divide the dough into two equal parts. Form each into a disc and wrap each disc separately in plastic wrap. Use your hands to then smooth over any cracks in the dough.
7. Place both discs in the fridge to chill for at least 40 minutes. When ready to use, remove from the fridge and let sit at room temperature until the dough becomes pliable yet is still cool. If it becomes too warm, return it to the fridge for a couple minutes.
8. To form a bottom crust, place one dough disc on a lightly floured surface and roll into a circle about ⅛ inch (0.25 cm) thick. Lightly sprinkle flour on your dough and rolling pin as needed to prevent sticking. Carefully wrap the dough circle around your rolling pin and unroll it across the top of a 9-inch (23-cm) pie plate. Press the sides and bottom to secure the dough to the pie plate. Fold the top edges under themselves and press down to secure.
9. To make a top crust, roll out the second dough disc the same way you did the first, and use according to your pie recipe's directions.

# GLUTEN FREE SINGLE PIE CRUST

*In my opinion, a good gluten free crust is one where others can't tell that it's gluten free! This recipe results in a tender yet crisp crust with a lightly salted flavor, so you can feel confident that everyone will enjoy your pie crust, whether they need to eat gluten free or not.*

**YIELD: 1 PIE CRUST**

**INGREDIENTS:**
- 1 ⅓ c. (213 g) gluten free all-purpose flour, plus more as needed
- ½ tsp. xanthan gum (omit if your flour already contains it)
- 1 Tbsp. (14 g) granulated sugar
- ½ tsp. salt
- ¼ tsp. baking powder
- ½ c. (77 g) vegetable shortening, plus more for greasing
- ⅓ c. (about 68 g) plain unsweetened non-dairy yogurt
- Ice water, as needed

**MAKE-AHEAD TIP:**
The dough disc can be made in advance and stored in the fridge for up to 5 days, or in the freezer wrapped in two layers of plastic wrap for up to 1 month.

**TO PAR-BAKE THE CRUST:**
Place the pie plate on a baking sheet and pierce the sides and bottom of the crust several times with a fork. Bake in a 375°F (approx. 190°C) oven for 12 minutes, rotating the plate halfway through.

**TO BLIND-BAKE THE CRUST:**
Place the pie plate on a baking sheet and pierce the sides and bottom of the crust several times with a fork. Bake in a 375°F (approx. 190°C) oven for 15–16 minutes, or until the edges are lightly browned and the sides and bottom appear to be fully cooked. Rotate the plate halfway through baking.

**INSTRUCTIONS:**

1. In the bowl of a food processor, combine the flour, xanthan gum, if using, sugar, salt, and baking powder. Pulse 8–10 times to mix.

2. Add the shortening one spoonful at a time, spreading the shortening pieces out rather than adding one big mound. Pulse 3–4 times, or until the shortening pieces appear to be pea-to bean-sized.

3. Add the yogurt and pulse again just a few times, until large clumps start to form but not all the flour is incorporated. If the dough seems really dry, add 1 Tbsp. of ice water and pulse once or twice more.

4. Turn the dough mixture out onto a flat, lightly floured surface. Gather the pieces of dough and knead a couple of times to incorporate the last bit of flour. Note: If the dough feels overly sticky, gently knead in a couple extra pinches of flour. If the dough feels overly dry, sprinkle with extra ice water a few drops at a time, all while aiming to handle the dough as little as possible.

5. Shape into a disc and wrap with plastic wrap. Smooth over the cracks as much as you can. Chill in the refrigerator for 1 hour.

6. Grease a 9-inch (about 23-cm) pie plate on the sides, bottom, and upper rim with shortening.

7. When ready to use it, remove the dough from the fridge and let sit at room temperature until it becomes pliable yet is still cool. If the dough becomes too warm, return it to the fridge for a couple of minutes. Remove the disc from the plastic wrap and place in the center of a sheet of parchment paper.

8. Roll out the dough to form a circle ⅛–¼ inch thick (about 0.5 cm), mending any cracks that form along the way.

9. Place your pie plate upside down in the center of the dough circle. Carefully slide your dominant hand under the parchment until you reach the center of the dough and plate, then quickly but carefully flip the plate and dough over right side up.

10. Slowly peel the parchment away and press the dough into the sides and bottom to secure it to the pie plate. Fold the top edges under themselves and press down to firmly secure to the rim of the pie plate. Crimp the edges as desired.

**NOTE:**
I find that gluten free all-purpose flours that list white rice flour as the first ingredient tend to work best in this recipe.

# GLUTEN FREE DOUBLE PIE CRUST

*When I'm in need of a double pie crust free of gluten, this recipe never lets me down. It holds together wonderfully and looks beautiful and enticing, but most important of all, it offers a wholesome and delicious flavor.*

YIELD: 2 PIE CRUSTS

INGREDIENTS:
- 2 ⅔ c. (426 g) gluten free all-purpose flour, plus more as needed
- 1 tsp. xanthan gum (omit if your flour already contains it)
- 2 Tbsp. (28 g) granulated sugar
- 1 tsp. salt
- ½ tsp. baking powder
- 1 c. (153 g) vegetable shortening, plus more for greasing
- ⅔ c. (about 136 g) plain unsweetened non-dairy yogurt
- Ice water, as needed

MAKE-AHEAD TIP:
The dough discs can be made in advance and stored in the fridge tightly wrapped in plastic wrap for up to 5 days, or in the freezer wrapped in two layers of plastic wrap for up to 1 month.

NOTE:
I find that gluten free all-purpose lours that list white rice flour as the first ingredient tend to work best in this recipe.

INSTRUCTIONS:
1. In the bowl of a food processor, combine the flour, xanthan gum, if using, sugar, salt, and baking powder. Pulse 8–10 times to mix.
2. Add the shortening one spoonful at a time, spreading the shortening pieces out rather than adding one big mound. Pulse 10–12 times, or until the shortening is mostly but not entirely incorporated. Scrape the sides and bottom of the bowl as needed.
3. Add the yogurt and pulse again 4–5 times until mostly but not entirely incorporated. If the dough seems really dry, add 1–2 Tbsp. of ice water and pulse once or twice more.
4. Turn the dough mixture out onto a flat, lightly floured surface. Gather the pieces of dough and knead a couple of times to incorporate the last bits of flour and yogurt. Note: If the dough feels overly sticky, gently knead in a couple extra pinches of flour. If the dough feels overly dry, sprinkle with extra ice water a few drops at a time, all while aiming to handle the dough as little as possible. Divide the dough into two equal parts. Form each into a disc and wrap in plastic wrap. Use your hands to then smooth over any cracks in the dough. Place both discs in the fridge to chill for at least 1 hour.
5. Grease a 9-inch (23-cm) pie plate on the sides, bottom, and upper rim with shortening.
6. To make a bottom crust, remove one disc from the fridge and let sit at room temperature until the dough becomes pliable yet is still cool. If it becomes too warm, return it to the fridge for a couple of minutes. Remove the disc from the plastic wrap and place in the center of a sheet of parchment paper.
7. Roll out the dough to form a circle ⅛–¼ inch thick (about 0.5 cm), mending any cracks that form along the way. Lightly sprinkle flour on the dough and rolling pin as needed to prevent sticking.
8. Place your pie plate upside down in the center of the dough circle. Carefully slide your dominant hand under the parchment until you reach the center of the dough and plate, then quickly but carefully flip the plate and dough over right side up.
9. Slowly peel the parchment away and press the dough into the sides and bottom to secure it to the pie plate. Fold the top edges under themselves and press down to secure the edges as well.
10. To make a top crust, roll out the second dough disc the same way you did the first, and use according to your pie recipe's directions.

# PUMPKIN PIE

*By far, my absolute favorite part of Thanksgiving is the pumpkin pie! Can you relate? After all, we're talking creamy custard pie loaded with warming spices, all settled perfectly in a tender, slightly crunchy and lightly salted crust. Top a slice with cool whipped cream and those tastebuds are in pumpkin pie heaven.*

YIELD: 8 SLICES

INGREDIENTS:

- 1 batch Single Pie Crust (page 94)
- 1 (15-oz. / 425-g) can pumpkin purée
- ⅔ c. (158 ml) canned coconut cream (shake well before opening and stir well before measuring)
- ⅓ c. + 2 Tbsp. (109 ml) unsweetened, unflavored non-dairy milk, such as almond, cashew, or soy
- ½ c. (108 g) packed light brown sugar
- ½ c. (115 g) granulated sugar
- ¼ c. (32 g) cornstarch
- 2 ½ tsp. pumpkin pie spice
- 1 tsp. vanilla extract
- ½ tsp. salt
- ¼ tsp. cinnamon

BEST GLUTEN FREE VERSION:
Use the Gluten Free Single Pie Crust recipe on page 96. Check the labels on all remaining ingredients to ensure they're gluten free as well.

MAKE-AHEAD TIP:
The pie is best if made 1 day before you plan to serve it.

INSTRUCTIONS:

1. Prepare the Single Pie Crust recipe and place the crust in a 9-inch (23-cm) pie plate. Par-bake according to the instructions on page 94. Set the crust aside and lower the oven temperature to 350°F (approx. 177°C).

2. Place all the remaining ingredients in a mixing bowl and gently whisk to combine. (Do not use a mixer or blender, or bubbles will form over the surface of the pie.) If there are any visible specks of coconut cream in the mixture, pinch with your fingers or remove them, otherwise they'll show up in the pie.

3. Pour the filling into the par-baked crust and smooth over the surface to pop any bubbles before baking.

4. Place the pie on a baking sheet for easier handling. Then transfer it to the oven and bake for 55–75 minutes, or until there's only a bit of jiggle left in the very center of the pie. Check at the 40-minute mark and tent the pie with foil if the edges are getting too dark.

5. Turn the oven off, but keep the pie in the oven. Crack the oven door several inches (or open it all the way if it won't stay cracked), and allow the pie to cool this way for at least an hour before transferring to a cooling rack. Once completely cooled, transfer the pie to the fridge to finish setting for at least 4 hours or overnight.

6. Remove the pie from the fridge 15 minutes before serving for a slightly chilled pie, or at least 1 hour prior to serving for room temperature.

7. Serve with whipped cream, if desired. Store leftover pie in the refrigerator.

# OLD FASHIONED PECAN PIE

*I'm just going to say it: this easy-to-make pie is a serious butterscotch pecan party in your mouth! It is so good that your guests won't believe it's vegan. In fact, my dad, who loves traditional pecan pie, is a big fan of this recipe.*

YIELD: 8 SERVINGS

INGREDIENTS:
- 1 batch Single Pie Crust (page 94)
- 1 ⅓ c. (316 ml) canned full-fat coconut milk (shake can well before opening and stir well before measuring)
- ¼ c. + 2 Tbsp. (48 g) cornstarch
- ¾ c. (162 g) packed light brown sugar
- ½ c. (119 ml) maple syrup
- ¼ c. (57 g) vegan butter or margarine
- ½ tsp. salt
- 1 Tbsp. (15 ml) bourbon (optional, but recommended)
- 2 tsp. vanilla extract
- 1 ¼ c. (150 g) pecan halves

FOR BEST GLUTEN FREE VERSION:
Use the recipe for a Gluten Free Single Pie Crust (page 96) and par-bake it at 350°F (approx. 177°C) for 12 minutes before adding the filling.

MAKE-AHEAD TIP:
This pie can be made 1 day in advance and stored at room temperature (away from heat) carefully tented with foil.

INSTRUCTIONS:
1. Prepare the Single Pie Crust recipe and place the crust in a 9-inch (23-cm) pie plate. Lay a sheet of plastic wrap flush against the raw crust to help prevent the dough from drying out, and store in the fridge until needed.
2. Preheat your oven to 350°F (approx. 177°C).
3. In a small mixing bowl, use a fork to whisk together the coconut milk and cornstarch until mostly smooth. Set aside for now.
4. In a saucepan over medium heat, combine the brown sugar, maple syrup, butter, and salt and whisk continuously until the butter is melted and it begins to simmer. Then turn the heat down to medium-low.
5. Add the coconut milk/cornstarch mixture and bourbon if using, and continue to whisk until completely smooth and the mixture just starts to thicken and bubble around the edges, 5–10 minutes. It's important that you continue whisking and never walk away during this process.
6. As soon as it starts to bubble, immediately remove the mixture from the heat and stir in the vanilla extract.
7. Pour the filling into your prepared pie crust.
8. Carefully place the whole pecans on the surface in any design you like. Alternatively, you can chop the pecans and sprinkle them evenly across the surface.
9. Place your pie on a baking sheet for easier handling. Then transfer it to the oven and bake for 35–45 minutes, or until it's very bubbly all over and there is very little jiggle in the center.
10. Remove the pie from the oven and place it on a cooling rack. Allow it to cool completely, about 4 hours, then place it in the fridge for at least 2 hours or overnight to help the filling become firm. It can then be removed and kept at room temperature until needed.

# COUNTRY APPLE PIE

*The perfect apple pie, in my opinion, is not subtle in any way—it needs to have enough sweetness and spice to give it a bold yet heavenly fall flavor, with just the slightest hint of lemon juice. This recipe for country apple pie is everything you'd hope for and then some.*

YIELD: 8–10 SERVINGS

INGREDIENTS:
- 1 batch Double Pie Crust (page 95)
- 3 ½ lb. (1590 g) apples (about 10 medium apples), peeled, cored, and sliced ⅛ inch (about 5 cm) thick
- ⅔ c. (153 g) granulated sugar, plus more for topping
- ⅓ c. (72 g) packed light brown sugar
- 3 Tbsp. (42 g) vegan butter or margarine
- 3 Tbsp. (26 g) all-purpose flour
- 1 Tbsp. (15 ml) lemon juice
- 1 ½ tsp. cinnamon
- ½ tsp. mace (optional but recommended)
- ¼ tsp. nutmeg
- Aquafaba (the liquid in a can of garbanzo beans; optional)

FOR BEST GLUTEN FREE VERSION:
Use the recipe for Gluten Free Double Pie Crust (page 97). Then, simply replace the all-purpose flour in the apple mixture with gluten free all-purpose flour or oat flour.

NOTES:
- Most prefer tart green apples such as Granny Smith for apple pies, but I like using a combination of sweet and tart apples in this recipe. Ultimately, any firm variety of apples will do.
- To keep the juices from oozing out, wait until the pie is completely cool before slicing. If you prefer warm pie, by all means, please serve it that way, but slices may be a bit looser.

INSTRUCTIONS:
1. Prepare the Double Pie Crust. Use one of the crusts to line a 9-inch (23-cm) pie plate, but do not crimp the edges just yet. Lay a sheet of plastic wrap flush against your raw crust to help prevent the dough from drying out. Keep the second disc wrapped in plastic wrap, and store both crusts in the fridge until needed.
2. Place the apple slices in a large pot and add all the remaining ingredients except the optional aquafaba.
3. Cook over medium-high heat, stirring frequently, until the apples are very steamy, slightly soft, and the juices start to thicken, 8–9 minutes. Meanwhile, remove both crusts from the fridge and remove the plastic wrap from the pie plate. Unwrap the second dough disc and place it on a lightly floured surface.
4. Transfer the hot apples to the pie plate and smooth over the surface so that the apples are evenly distributed.
5. Roll out your second disc of pie dough the same way you did the first. Wrap it around your rolling pin and carefully transfer it to cover the apples.
6. Tuck the edges of the top crust under the edges of the bottom crust and press down to secure them to the pie plate rim. Crimp the edges to create a fun design, or leave as-is for a more rustic look.
7. Cover the pie in plastic wrap and place in the fridge to chill for 1 hour.
8. When ready to bake, remove the pie from the fridge, place a baking rack in the center of your oven, and preheat the oven to 400°F (approx. 204°C). Once the oven is ready, set your pie on a baking sheet. Create five to six 2-inch (5-cm) slits in the top crust. (I usually do a star-like design right in the center.) If you want your crust to have a slightly shiny "egg wash" look, apply a very light coating of aquafaba to the surface. Top with a couple of generous pinches of granulated sugar (even if you left off the aqua faba).
9. Bake on the middle rack for 50–55 minutes. Check the pie at the 40-minute mark. If you feel the crust is getting too dark, lightly tent the pie with foil.
10. Allow the pie to cool on a cooling rack for at least 30 minutes before slicing. (See second note to the left.) Serve with non-dairy vanilla ice cream, if desired.

MAKE-AHEAD TIP:
You can bake your pie 1 day in advance. Once completely cool, lightly tent it with foil and store on your countertop away from heat until needed.

# CHOCOLATE CREAM PIE WITH CHOCOLATE COOKIE CRUST

*Creamy, cool, rich chocolate pie in a lightly salted chocolate cookie crust—there isn't a single member of our family that doesn't absolutely love this pie. If you prefer your chocolate cream pie with a traditional crust, by all means, please make it with a blind-baked Single Pie Crust (page 94). You can't go wrong either way.*

YIELD: 8 SERVINGS

INGREDIENTS:

**Chocolate Cookie Crust:**
- 26 chocolate cream-filled sandwich cookies (about 300 g)
- ⅓ c. (75 g) vegan butter or margarine, melted

**Chocolate Cream Filling:**
- ½ c. (119 ml) unsweetened, unflavored non-dairy milk such as almond, cashew, or soy
- ½ c. (64 g) cornstarch
- 3 c. (711 ml) canned full-fat coconut milk (shake cans well before opening and stir well before measuring)
- ¾ c. + 1 Tbsp. (187 g) granulated sugar
- ½ tsp. salt
- ½ tsp. vanilla extract
- 1 ¾ c. mini dairy-free chocolate chips (325 g) or regular-sized dairy-free chocolate chips (315 g), plus more for topping
- Vegan whipped cream for topping (optional)

**FOR BEST GLUTEN FREE VERSION:**
In the crust, use gluten free chocolate cream-filled sandwich cookies.

**MAKE-AHEAD TIP:**
This pie can be made 1 day in advance and stored uncovered in the refrigerator. Remove from the fridge 10 minutes before serving.

INSTRUCTIONS:

1. Place the chocolate sandwich cookies (cream filling and all) and melted butter in your food processor and blend until the cookies become sandy. Alternatively, you can place the cookies in a large resealable plastic bag, press the air out, and crush the cookies with a rolling pin or other heavy object. Some remaining pea-sized pieces of cookie are ok. Afterward, pour the melted butter into the bag and shake it all together.

2. Pour the cookie mixture into a 9-inch (23-cm) pie plate and use your fingers to evenly spread and press the mixture on the bottom and up the sides to create the crust. Place in the refrigerator to chill until needed.

3. Combine the non-dairy milk and cornstarch in a small bowl and whisk with a fork until smooth. Set this aside for now as well.

4. In a large saucepan, combine the coconut milk, sugar, salt, and vanilla. Set over medium heat and whisk frequently until the mixture starts to bubble around the edges, 8–10 minutes.

5. At this point, slowly add the chocolate chips while whisking until all the chocolate is melted and incorporated.

6. Slowly add the milk/cornstarch mixture while whisking vigorously. Continue whisking until the chocolate cream becomes thick, 2–5 minutes.

7. Remove from the heat and quickly transfer the chocolate cream to the prepared pie crust. Note: Only use what easily comes out of the saucepan; do not scrape the bottom of the pot or you may end up with lumps in your pie. Gently smooth over the surface of the pie with the back of a spoon or a rubber spatula.

8. Allow the pie to cool at room temperature for 30–40 minutes before transferring to the refrigerator to chill completely, about 6 hours, or until the bottom of the pan feels cold to the touch.

9. Just before serving, top the pie with whipped cream and extra chocolate chips, if desired.

# EASY SKILLET APPLE CRISP

*This apple crisp is loaded with tender cinnamon apples and topped with a chewy oatmeal topping. And even better, it's made and served in a cast iron skillet, which brings the presentation factor through the roof!*

YIELD: ABOUT 10 SERVINGS

INGREDIENTS:

### Apple Filling:
- 2 lb. (907 g) apples, chopped into ½–1-inch (1–3-cm) chunks (about 6 medium apples)
- ¾ c. (173 g) granulated sugar
- 2 Tbsp. (18 g) all-purpose flour or (14 g) oat flour
- 1 tsp. cinnamon
- 1 Tbsp. (15 ml) lemon juice

### Cinnamon Oat Topping:
- 1 ⅓ c. (149 g) rolled old-fashioned oats
- ⅓ c. (47 g) all-purpose flour or (36 g) oat flour
- ⅓ c. + 1 Tbsp. (86 g) granulated sugar
- ⅓ c. (35 g) chopped pecans (optional, but recommended)
- 1 ½ tsp. cinnamon
- ½ c. (113 g) vegan butter or margarine, softened, plus more for greasing

### FOR BEST GLUTEN FREE VERSION:
Use the oat flour option in both the filling and topping. Alternatively, you can use gluten free all-purpose flour. Make sure the oats and oat flour you're using are certified gluten free.

### MAKE-AHEAD TIP:
This apple crisp is best when served the same day it is baked. However, the apples can be chopped and stored in an airtight container or resealable plastic storage bag 1 day in advance.

INSTRUCTIONS:

1. Preheat your oven to 350°F (approx. 177°C). Grease a 10-inch (25-cm) or 12-inch (30-cm) cast iron skillet (or any other 2–2.5-quart dish) with butter. Set it aside for now.
2. Combine all the ingredients for the apple filling in a medium-sized mixing bowl and stir well to combine. Transfer to your prepared skillet or baking dish.
3. Using the same unwashed mixing bowl, combine all of the topping ingredients until the butter is well incorporated.
4. Sprinkle the topping evenly over the surface of the apple filling.
5. Bake for 40–50 minutes, or until the crisp bubbles around the edges and the tips of the topping start to lightly brown. Let it cool at least 5–10 minutes. Serve with non-dairy vanilla ice cream or whipped cream, if desired.

NOTES:

- I prefer a sweeter apple variety in this recipe rather than tart, but either type will do! Aim for roughly 1-inch (3-cm) chunks when chopping your apples. I do this by first cutting my apples into thick slices, and then chopping each slice into thirds. Peeling is optional, but I usually leave the peel on for this recipe.
- Baking in a 10-inch (25-cm) skillet or 2-quart dish will result in a taller, heartier apple crisp, whereas using a 12-inch (30-cm) skillet or 2.5-quart dish will result in a shallower, more spread-out apple crisp. You can't go wrong either way; both are delicious!

# SWEET POTATO PIE WITH CINNAMON SUGARED PECANS

*The best words to describe this recipe would be pure and delicious. The sweet potato filling is free of flours and starches, ensuring each bite offers the flavor and texture of whipped sweet potatoes combined beautifully with brown sugar and spices. Adorn the outer edge of this pie with chopped cinnamon sugared pecans to offer a scrumptious crunch with the last few bites of each slice.*

YIELD: 8 SLICES

INGREDIENTS:

### Sweet Potato Pie
- 1 ½ lb. (680 g) yams or other orange-colored sweet potatoes
- 1 batch Single Pie Crust (page 95)
- ⅔ c. (158 ml) unsweetened, unflavored non-dairy milk such as almond, cashew, or soy
- ⅓ c. + 1 Tbsp. (94 ml) canned coconut cream (shake well before opening and stir well before measuring)
- ⅓ c. + 1 Tbsp. (85 g) vegan butter or margarine, room temperature
- 1 tsp. vanilla extract
- ¾ c. (162 g) packed light brown sugar
- ¼ c. (58 g) granulated sugar
- ¾ tsp. cinnamon
- ½ tsp. nutmeg
- ¼ tsp. ground ginger
- ¼ tsp. salt

### Cinnamon Sugared Pecans
- Oil for greasing
- ½ c. (115 g) granulated sugar
- 1 tsp. cinnamon
- ¼ tsp. salt
- 2 Tbsp. (30 ml) aquafaba (the liquid in a can of garbanzo beans)
- 1 tsp. vanilla extract
- 2 c. (240 g) pecan halves

INSTRUCTIONS:

1. Preheat your oven to 375°F (approx. 190°C). Pierce each potato 3–4 times with a fork. Bake on a parchment-lined or nonstick baking sheet until juice oozes from the potatoes and they're very soft. This could take anywhere from 45–90 minutes, depending on the size of the potatoes.

2. Prepare the Single Pie Crust recipe and place the crust in a 9-inch (23-cm) pie plate. Par-bake according to the instructions on page 94. Set the crust aside and reduce the oven temperature to 350°F (approx. 177°C).

3. Scoop out the flesh of the sweet potatoes (there should be slightly more than 2 c.) and place it in a medium mixing bowl. Mash with a potato masher until mostly smooth.

4. Add all the remaining sweet potato pie ingredients to the bowl. Using a handheld or stand mixer, blend the mixture until well combined and mostly smooth. Note: You may see small specks of butter throughout this mixture and that's ok! They will melt and disappear during baking.

5. Pour the filling into the prepared pie crust and smooth over the surface. Place on a baking sheet for easier handling. Bake until the filling has puffed up slightly and there's only a small amount of jiggle, 40–50 minutes.

6. Turn the oven off but keep the pie in the oven. Crack the oven door several inches (or open it all the way if it won't stay cracked). Allow the pie to cool this way for at least an hour before transferring to a cooling rack. Once completely cooled, transfer the pie to the fridge to finish setting for at least 4 hours or overnight.

7. To make the cinnamon sugared pecans, preheat your oven to 250°F (approx. 120°C). Grease a baking sheet liberally with oil. (Do not use parchment paper for this one, only a greased baking sheet.)

Recipe continues

**FOR BEST GLUTEN FREE VERSION:**
Use the Gluten Free Single Pie Crust recipe on page 96. Check the labels on all remaining ingredients to ensure they're gluten free as well.

**MAKE-AHEAD TIP:**
The pie is best if made 1 day before you plan to serve it.

8. In a small bowl, combine the granulated sugar, cinnamon, and salt. Set aside.

9. Combine the aquafaba and vanilla in a mixing bowl and whisk vigorously until frothy, about 1 minute. Add the pecans to the bowl and stir to evenly coat each and every nut.

10. Sprinkle the sugar mixture over the pecans and stir until evenly distributed and there is very little sugar left in the bowl.

11. Spread the pecans in a single layer on the prepared baking sheet. Bake for 1 hour, stirring nuts every 15 minutes (for a total of three times before removing from the oven).

12. Once the nuts are completely cooled, chop just half of the pecans into pea- to bean-sized pieces and sprinkle a generous amount along the outer edge of the cooled sweet potato pie, creating a border about 1 ½ inches (4 cm) wide all around the edge. Decide if you'd like to chop and add more pecans. Otherwise, save the leftovers for later or serve them in a candy dish on the dessert table! Return the pie to the fridge.

13. Remove the pie from the fridge 10–15 minutes before serving time. Serve with whipped cream, if desired. Store leftover pie in the refrigerator.

# CARAMEL APPLE CRUMBLE SLAB PIE

*If you're looking for a showstopping dessert that serves a crowd, look no further! This caramel apple crumble slab pie is not only grand and gorgeous in appearance, it's loaded with a variety of delicious flavors and textures, as well. Be sure to serve it warm and topped with ice cream to really blow everyone away.*

**YIELD: 15–20 SERVINGS**

**INGREDIENTS:**

**Apple Pie Base:**
- 1 batch Double Pie Crust (page 95), formed into one large disc instead of two
- Vegan butter or margarine for greasing
- 3 ½ lb. (1590 g) Granny Smith apples (about 10 medium apples)
- ⅔ c. (153 g) granulated sugar
- ⅓ c. (47 g) all-purpose flour
- 1 tsp. cinnamon
- ¼ tsp. ginger
- ¼ tsp. allspice

**Crumble Topping:**
- 1 c. (105 g) quick-cooking oats
- 1 c. (216 g) packed light brown sugar
- ½ c. (70 g) all-purpose flour
- ¼ tsp. cinnamon
- ½ c. (113 g) cold vegan butter or margarine, cut into ½-inch (about 1.5-cm) cubes

**Caramel Drizzle:**
- ½ c. (108 g) packed light brown sugar
- ¼ c. (59 ml) canned coconut cream
- 1 tsp. vanilla extract
- Pinch of salt

**INSTRUCTIONS:**

1. Prepare the Double Pie Crust, form into one large disc, and chill, wrapped in plastic wrap, for at least 30 minutes.

2. Grease a 15-x-10-inch (38-x-25-cm) baking sheet with butter. Set aside for now. Preheat your oven to 375°F (approx. 190°C).

3. On a large, lightly floured surface, roll the dough to create a rectangle approximately 17 x 12 inches (43 x 30 cm) in size. Carefully wrap the dough around your rolling pin and unroll it across your prepared baking sheet. Gently press the dough into all the edges and corners and along the bottom of the pan. Then fold the dough edges under themselves along the top rim of the sheet and crimp as desired. Cover the entire sheet with plastic wrap and place in the refrigerator until needed.

4. Peel, core, and slice the apples into ⅛–¼-inch-thick (about 0.25–0.5-cm) slices. Place in a large mixing bowl along with the granulated sugar, flour, cinnamon, ginger, and allspice. Toss until the apples are evenly coated. Transfer the apples to the prepared crust and spread until they reach all the corners and sides.

5. To make the crumble topping, combine the oats, brown sugar, flour, and cinnamon in the same large, unwashed bowl. Stir to combine. Using a pastry cutter, a large fork, or your fingertips, cut in the butter until the mixture resembles large crumbs. Evenly sprinkle over the surface of the apples.

6. Bake the slab pie for 45 minutes, or until the apples are fork-tender. Check on the pie at the 30-minute mark, and if the crust is looking too dark, loosely top with foil for the remainder of the time.

Recipe continues

**FOR BEST GLUTEN FREE VERSION:**
Make the recipe for Gluten Free Double Pie Crust (page 97) and use gluten free all-purpose flour in the apple pie base and crumble topping.

7. Meanwhile, make the caramel drizzle. Combine all the ingredients in a small saucepan and cook over medium-low to medium heat. Whisk gently until the caramel starts to slightly thicken, 7–10 minutes. Turn off the heat. The caramel will continue to thicken as it cools.

8. Cool the slab pie for at least 10 minutes, drizzling the caramel over the top just before serving. This pie is magical when served fresh and hot out of the oven. Serve with non-dairy vanilla ice cream, if desired.

**MAKE-AHEAD TIPS:**
• The entire slab pie can be assembled (but not baked), covered in plastic wrap, and stored in the refrigerator up to 3 days in advance. The day you're ready for it, transfer to room temperature 1 hour before baking.

• Alternatively, the slab pie can be baked 1 day in advance. Once it is completely cool, cover in foil and store at room temperature away from heat. Enjoy as-is, or warm the slab pie in a 350°F (approx. 177°C) oven for 15 minutes before serving.

• The caramel drizzle can be made up to 5 days in advance and stored in a mason jar or other airtight container in the refrigerator. Warm in the microwave or in a saucepan on the stove just before drizzling.

# BUTTERMILK CUSTARD PIE

*This cool and creamy custard pie with tender crust will satisfy the purists in your group. Aside from its modest tang and hint of nutmeg, this pie is classically simple in the most delicious way possible.*

YIELD: 8

INGREDIENTS:
- 1 batch Single Pie Crust (page 94)
- 1 ¼ c. (288 g) granulated sugar
- ⅓ c. (43 g) cornstarch
- ½ tsp. salt
- ¼ tsp. nutmeg, plus more for topping
- Generous pinch of turmeric
- 1 (16-oz. / 454-g) package silken tofu, drained
- ¾ c. (177 ml) canned coconut cream (shake well before opening and stir well before measuring)
- 1 Tbsp. (15 ml) white distilled vinegar
- 2 tsp. vanilla extract

FOR BEST GLUTEN FREE VERSION:
Use the Gluten Free Single Pie Crust recipe on page 96. Check the labels on all remaining ingredients to ensure they're gluten free as well.

MAKE-AHEAD TIP:
The pie is best if made 1 day before you plan to serve it.

INSTRUCTIONS:

1. Prepare the Single Pie Crust recipe and place the crust in a 9-inch (23-cm) pie plate. Par-bake according to the instructions on page 94. Set the crust aside and keep the oven on at 400°F (approx. 204°C).

2. In a medium mixing bowl, stir together the sugar, cornstarch, salt, nutmeg, and turmeric. Set aside.

3. In the bowl of a food processor, combine the tofu, coconut cream, vinegar, and vanilla and blend until very smooth.

4. Transfer the tofu mixture to the bowl containing the dry ingredients and stir well to combine.

5. Place your pie plate on a baking sheet for easier handling. Pour the custard mixture into the prepared crust and bake for 45–50 minutes, or until the edges are very puffy and only the center jiggles. Turn the oven off but keep the pie in the oven. Crack the oven door several inches (or open it all the way if it won't stay cracked). Allow the pie to cool this way for at least an hour before transferring to a cooling rack. Once completely cooled, transfer the pie to the fridge to finish setting for at least 4 hours or overnight.

6. Remove the pie from the fridge 15 minutes before serving time for a slightly chilled pie, or one hour prior to serving for room-temperature pie. When ready to serve, sprinkle the surface of the pie with ground nutmeg and serve with whipped cream, if you like. Store leftovers in the fridge.

# BOURBON PECAN CHOCOLATE PIE

*Chocolate lovers, get ready—this pie is for you! We're talking a fudgy chocolate center, spiked with a bit of bourbon and swirled and topped with a generous amount of toasted chopped pecans. This pie is insanely good and so much fun to eat.*

YIELD: 8

INGREDIENTS:
- 1 batch Single Pie Crust (page 94)
- 1 ⅓ c. (316 ml) canned full-fat coconut milk (shake can well before opening and stir well before measuring)
- ⅓ c. + 1 Tbsp. (48 g) cornstarch
- ¾ c. (162 g) packed light brown sugar
- ⅓ c. (79 ml) maple syrup
- ¼ c. (57 g) vegan butter or margarine
- ½ tsp. salt
- 3 oz. (86 g) 85% dark chocolate, roughly chopped
- 2 Tbsp. (30 ml) bourbon
- 1 ¾ c. (210 g) pecans, chopped, divided

FOR BEST GLUTEN FREE VERSION:
Use the Gluten Free Single Pie Crust recipe on page 96. Check the labels on all remaining ingredients to ensure they're gluten free as well.

MAKE-AHEAD TIP:
The pie is best if made 1 day before you plan to serve it.

INSTRUCTIONS:
1. Prepare the Single Pie Crust recipe and place the crust in a 9-inch (23-cm) pie plate. Par-bake according to the instructions on page 94. Set the crust aside and reduce the oven temperature to 350°F (approx. 177°C).

2. In a small bowl, whisk together the coconut milk and cornstarch thoroughly with a fork until mostly smooth.

3. In a medium saucepan over medium heat, combine the brown sugar, maple syrup, butter, and salt. Whisk continuously until the butter is melted and the mixture begins to simmer.

4. Slowly add the coconut milk mixture while whisking, followed by the chopped chocolate and bourbon. Continue whisking until the mixture becomes thick and starts to bubble, 5–10 minutes. Immediately remove from the heat and stir in 1 ¼ c. (150 g) of the chopped pecans.

5. Pour the filling into the prepared crust, being careful not to scrape the filling from the bottom of the saucepan, as this will likely add clumps to your filling. Just use what easily pours out of the saucepan. Sprinkle the remaining ½ c. (60 g) pecans evenly over the surface.

6. Place the pie on a baking sheet for easier handling. Bake for 40–50 minutes, or until there are little bubbles forming all over the surface and it appears slightly puffed up all over. Check the pie at the 30-minute mark and loosely tent with foil if the crust is starting to get too dark.

7. Remove the pie from the oven, but keep it on the hot baking sheet for the first hour of cooling. Then transfer to a cooling rack. Once completely cooled, chill the pie in the fridge for at least 4 hours or overnight to finish setting. Afterward, the pie can be kept at room temperature away from heat loosely tented with foil until ready to serve. Top with whipped cream, if desired.

# FRENCH VANILLA ICE CREAM

*The only thing better than offering your Thanksgiving desserts with vanilla ice cream is offering your desserts with homemade vanilla ice cream! Everyone will be so impressed, mark my words.*

YIELD: ABOUT 8 SERVINGS

INGREDIENTS:
- 1 c. (127 g) unsalted raw cashews (see note)
- 1 (13.5-oz. / 398-ml) can coconut cream
- ⅓ c. + 2 Tbsp. (101 g) granulated sugar
- ⅓ c. (79 ml) maple syrup
- 2 ½ tsp. vanilla extract
- ¼ tsp. salt

FOR BEST GLUTEN FREE VERSION:
This recipe is naturally gluten free, but check all ingredient labels to be sure.

MAKE-AHEAD TIP:
This ice cream can be made and stored in the freezer for about 4 weeks (if not longer), but I feel it's best if enjoyed within the first 2 weeks.

INSTRUCTIONS:
1. Place your cashews in a small bowl and completely cover with water. Soak the cashews for at least 6 hours, but no longer than 24 hours. (If soaking longer than 6 hours, place cashews in the fridge until you're ready for them.) Meanwhile, if needed, place the base for your ice cream maker in the freezer to chill.
2. Drain and thoroughly rinse your cashews and place them in a high-speed blender. Add all the remaining ingredients to the blender as well.
3. Blend on high speed until the mixture is completely smooth and liquified.
4. Transfer this mixture to your ice cream maker and churn according to the manufacturer's directions until the ice cream is very thick, about 45 minutes.
5. Transfer the ice cream to an airtight container and store in the freezer for at least 2 hours to continue to harden.

NOTE:
If you don't have an ultra-high-speed blender such as a Vitamix, I recommend substituting an additional 1 c. (237 ml) of canned coconut cream for the cashews.

# CLASSIC WHIPPED CREAM

*Can you name one dessert that isn't brought to another level of delicious by adding whipped cream? Nope, me neither! This recipe is simple and perfectly sweet, allowing your desserts to be the true star of the plate. Make your whipped cream the day before to ensure the perfect consistency.*

YIELD: ABOUT 1 ½ CUPS WHIPPED CREAM

INGREDIENTS:

- 2 (13.5-oz. / 400-ml) cans coconut cream (or 4 small cans), chilled in the refrigerator for at least 6 hours or overnight.
- ⅔ c. (87 g) powdered sugar (confectioners' sugar)

MAKE-AHEAD TIP:

This whipped cream can be made in advance and stored in the fridge for about 2 weeks or in the freezer for 1 month. Thaw frozen whipped cream at room temperature for 20 minutes or in the refrigerator for several hours before serving.

INSTRUCTIONS:

1. Remove the coconut cream from the fridge and scoop out 1 ¼ c. (276 g) of the thick coconut cream from the top. Avoid the watery liquid as much as you can. Place the cream in a mixing bowl. Note: You may only need to open one can.

2. Add the powdered sugar to the bowl.

3. Using a handheld or stand mixer, mix on medium-low until smooth and fluffy. Scrape the sides and bottom of the bowl as needed. The whipped cream can be used immediately, but for slightly thicker whipped cream, place in the freezer for 15 minutes or in the refrigerator for at least 1 hour or until needed.

NOTES:

- Give your whipped cream more of an ice cream texture by placing it in the freezer for at least 2 hours. Allow it to sit at room temperature for 5–10 minutes before serving.

- It's usually best to chill one extra can of coconut cream for backup, as every once in a great while, you'll end up with coconut cream that doesn't set when chilled.

# INDEX